Italian Gelateria - Ice Cream Shop

Complete Guide to Creating and Managing a Successful Gelateria

I0446317

Delicious Dreams Gelato:

Preface Dear reader, It is with immense pleasure and a touch of sweet anticipation that I welcome you to "Artisan Gelato: From the Perfect Base to Success Strategies." This manual was born out of love for the art of creating delicious gelato and a passion for sharing knowledge that goes beyond the mere preparation of a dessert. The idea for this manual took shape in the desire to offer you a complete guide, a reliable resource that accompanies you through every phase of your journey into the fascinating and flavorful world of artisan gelato. Whether you are an aspiring gelato maker, a cooking enthusiast, or simply a taste explorer, I hope you will find inspiration, valuable information, and a generous dose of creativity within these pages. The Journey Begins with the Perfect Base We will start from the base, literally and figuratively. Creating delicious gelato begins with the right ingredients and a deep understanding of the preparation process. Together, we will explore the secrets to achieving the perfect taste, from selecting high-quality ingredients to mixing and freezing techniques that will transform your base into a creamy masterpiece. From the Kitchen to the Heart of the Community But our journey does not stop in the kitchen. We will traverse the heart of your community, exploring innovative marketing strategies, ways to engage the public, and creating an unforgettable taste experience. We will see how your gelateria can become not only a place of delight but also a community meeting point through events, collaborations, and a sustainable approach. From Craftsmanship to Innovation: A Personal Touch Artisan gelato goes beyond simple production. It will be your signature, your personal touch that makes your product unique. We will explore how to create a distinctive brand, tackle common industry challenges, and innovate with new flavors and creative techniques. I hope this manual inspires you to pursue your dreams in the world of artisan gelato, providing you with the knowledge to face challenges and the resources to celebrate successes. The road may be sweet, and with the right mix of passion, knowledge, and creativity, your journey will undoubtedly be delightful. Whether you are starting your journey or honing your skills, I wish you a frozen adventure rich in satisfaction and achievements. Happy journey into the world of artisan gelato! With Flavor, Nuccio Longardi

Main Chapters:

1. **Introduction to Artisan Gelato**: •

   Discover what makes the art of creating delicious gelato unique. Take a look at the historical roots and evolution of artisan gelato.

2. **Creating Dreams and Goals:** •

   Deepen your dreams of opening a gelateria and turn them into tangible goals. Understand the importance of having a clear vision for success.

3. **The Perfect Taste:** •

   Explore the selection of high-quality ingredients and discover how they influence the flavor of your gelato. Delve into techniques for achieving the perfect taste.

4. **Store Design:** •

   From the early stages of setting up your space to creating a welcoming and inviting atmosphere. Discover the importance of design in presenting your product.

5. **Taste Marketing Strategies:** •

Learn how to make yourself known in your community. Explore marketing strategies to attract customers hungry for sweetness. Deepen the use of online channels and social media.

6. **Creativity in the Production Process:** •

  Reveal the process of creating unique flavors. Experiment with new tastes and learn to stand out through innovation.

7. **Staff Management:** •

  Build a passionate team and involve them in your vision. Discover strategies for effectively managing staff.

8. **Adaptation to Seasons and Holidays:** •

  Customize your offerings for different seasons and holidays to attract new customers. Explore creative ideas to keep your menu fresh.

9. **Palate Education and Quality:** •

  Learn how to educate customers about your artisan gelato and make them appreciate quality. Deepen the importance of palate education.

10. **Social Media and Community:** •

  Deepen how to use online channels to connect with your community and promote your gelateria. Include specific strategies and tips for creating engaging content.

11. **Sustainability and Environmental Impact:** •

Explore sustainable practices to reduce the environmental impact of your business. Share how your gelateria can be part of positive change.

12.Creating a Distinctive Brand: •

Add a personal touch to your gelateria. Discover how to create a brand that stands out in the competitive market.

13.Events and Collaborations: •

Engage your community through events and collaborations with other local businesses. Explore successful examples and effective strategies.

14.Tackling Common Challenges: •

Face common challenges in the gelato industry and discover practical solutions. Share case study examples to inspire and guide.

15.Collection of Italian Recipes: •

Delve into the Italian culinary heritage with authentic and delicious gelato recipes to enrich your menu.

Conclusions: This manual is designed to be a comprehensive resource, from theory to practice, that will guide you through every aspect of managing a successful artisan gelateria. We hope these pages inspire your creativity and assist you in achieving your goals in the world of artisan gelato. Happy reading and success in your frozen adventure!

Bibliography

1. **"The Perfect Scoop:** Ice Creams, Sorbets, Granitas, and Sweet Accompaniments" by David Lebovitz - A comprehensive guide to crafting artisanal ice creams with delightful recipes.

2. **"Start Your Own Ice** Cream Truck Business: Step-By-Step Guide to Success" by Danielle Buchanan - A practical resource for anyone looking to start a mobile ice cream business.

3. **"Gelato Business**: Start and Operate a Successful Gelato Shop" by Lisa Couture - Practical advice for launching and managing a successful gelateria.

4. **"How to Open** a Financially Successful Ice Cream & Frozen Yogurt Shop" by Anthony T. Smith - Insights into the financial and managerial aspects of running an ice cream shop.

5. **"The Gelato Maker's Guide**: A Simple, Fun Approach to Making Artisan Gelato at Home" by Morgan Morano - Ideal for those who want to experiment with crafting artisan gelato at home.

6. **"Marketing Your Gelato Business" by Lee Raito** - Practical tips for implementing effective marketing strategies for a gelateria.

7. **"Gelato History and Recipes:** The Origins and History of Gelato With 80 Authentic Italian Recipes" by Alessandro Scappini - A historical perspective on gelato with authentic Italian recipes.

8. **"The Business of Food**: Encyclopedia of the Food and Drink Industries" by Gary Allen - An encyclopedia providing a comprehensive overview of the food industry, including that of ice creams.

9. **"Sweet Cream and Sugar** Cones: 90 Recipes for Making Your Own Ice Cream and Frozen Treats from Bi-Rite Creamery" by Kris Hoogerhyde, Anne Walker, and Dabney Gough - Artisanal recipes from one of the most famous creameries in San Francisco.

10. **"Gelato, Ice Creams & Sorbets" by Linda** Tubby - A collection of recipes for ice creams, sorbets, and creams to be made at home.

Chapter 1: Introduction Welcome to the fascinating world of gelato. Let's explore together what makes the art of creating delicious ice creams unique.

Chapter 2: Dreams and Aspirations • Let's delve into your dreams of opening a gelateria and how to turn them into tangible goals.

Chapter 3: The Perfect Taste • We'll explore the selection of high-quality ingredients and how they influence the flavor of your gelato.

Chapter 4: Store Design • Take the first steps in setting up your space. Learn how to create a welcoming and inviting atmosphere.

Chapter 5: Taste Marketing • Marketing strategies to make yourself known in your community. Discover how to attract customers hungry for sweetness.

Chapter 6: The Creative Process • Let's reveal the process of creating unique flavors and experimenting with new tastes.

Chapter 7: Staff Management • How to build a passionate team and involve them in your vision.

Chapter 8: The Magic of Seasons • Adapt your offerings to different seasons and festivities to attract new customers.

Chapter 9: Palate Education • How to educate customers about your artisanal gelato and make them appreciate its quality.

Chapter 10: Social Media and Community • Utilize online channels to connect with your community and promote your gelateria.

Chapter 11: Sustainability • Explore sustainable practices to reduce the environmental impact of your business.

Chapter 12: Personal Touch • Add a unique touch to your gelateria. Learn how to create a brand that stands out.

Chapter 13: Events and Collaborations • Engage your community through events and collaborations with other local businesses.

Chapter 14: Facing Common Challenges • Address common challenges in the gelato industry and discover practical solutions.

Chapter 15: Collection of Italian Flavored Ice Cream Recipes • Delve into the Italian culinary heritage with a selection of authentic and delightful recipes to enrich your menu

Chapter 1: Introduction

Welcome to the captivating world of gelato! In this introductory chapter, we will explore the fundamental concepts that will form the foundation for your adventure in creating and managing a successful gelateria.

Chapter Objectives:

1. Presentation: Let's delve into the emotion and passion behind the opening of a gelateria.

2. Overview: We provide an overview of the key themes covered in the book.

3. Importance of the Art of Gelato: We delve into the significant tradition of crafting artisanal gelato.

Key Contents: 1.1 The Charm of Gelato: • Explore the unique role that gelato plays in culinary and social culture.

1.2 The Path That Awaits You: •

Discuss the exciting journey you will embark on in the world of gelateria. 1.3 The Inspiration Behind the Book: • Share the motivations and goals behind the creation of this guide.

Personal Reflections: Brief personal reflections will be inserted to provide a human touch and share meaningful experiences related to the opening of a gelateria.

Begin your culinary journey into the gelateria with the right dose of inspiration and preparation. Happy reading!

Strengths: The first chapter stands out for several strengths that will capture the reader's attention and engage them in the fascinating world of the gelateria.

1.1 Exploration of Emotion: •
Vivid Description: We use vivid descriptions to convey the emotion and passion surrounding the opening of a gelateria, stimulating the reader's imagination. • Engaging Anecdotes: Introducing engaging anecdotes and personal stories can make the experience more tangible and relatable to the reader.

1.2 Detailed Overview: •
Logical Organization: We present a detailed overview of the themes covered in the book, logically organized to facilitate understanding of the entrepreneurial journey. • Curiosity Aroused: We pique the reader's curiosity by offering glimpses of topics that will be explored in the subsequent chapters.

1.3 Importance of the Art of Gelato: •
Elevating the Meaning: We delve into the significance of the art of gelato, elevating it from a simple product to a cultural and culinary experience. • Appeal to Tradition: Connecting the art of gelato to culinary traditions enhances its intrinsic value and makes it part of a broader heritage.

Captivating Personal Reflections: • Invitation to Interaction: We encourage reader interaction through dedicated spaces for personal reflections, urging them to connect emotionally with the material. • Empathetic Perspective: We create an empathetic perspective, demonstrating understanding of the challenges and emotions the reader may face on their journey.

In summary, the initial chapter offers an engaging experience, channeling enthusiasm and passion for the gelateria and providing a solid foundation for exploring subsequent topics.

Weaknesses: Despite the careful design of the introductory chapter, some areas that could benefit from further improvement can be identified.

1.1 Exploration of Emotion: •

Variation in Tone: It might be useful to vary the emotional tone to ensure that the emotion is conveyed more broadly, engaging a wider range of readers. • Need for More Details: Some sections could benefit from more details or tangible examples to make the experience of opening a gelateria more concrete.

1.2 Detailed Overview: •

Information Overload: While an overview is essential, there is a risk of providing too much information in this first chapter, potentially overwhelming the reader. • Balancing Curiosity: Care must be taken to maintain a balance between arousing the reader's curiosity and not revealing too much, maintaining interest for subsequent chapters.

1.3 Importance of the Art of Gelato: •

Cultural Aspect Deepening: A deeper exploration of the cultural aspect related to the art of gelato could be beneficial, more closely linking it to everyday life experiences. • Greater Clarity on Art: Further clarification on what makes the art of gelato unique and how it influences the creation of an extraordinary culinary experience.

Captivating Personal Reflections: • More Structured Guide: To optimize reader interaction, it might be helpful to provide a more structured guide for personal reflections, making reader participation easier. • Empathy Promotion: Making empathy promotion more evident by explicitly inviting the reader to step into the shoes of a gelato entrepreneur.

Despite these weaknesses, each aspect can be improved with careful revision and targeted attention.

Examples and Case Studies: To further enrich the introductory chapter, we could incorporate examples and case studies that tangibly highlight the emotion and passion behind the opening of a gelateria.

1.1 Exploration of Emotion: •

Example 1: Marco's Journey and His Artisan Gelateria • Narrate the exciting journey of Marco, a gelato enthusiast who turned his passion into an artisan gelateria. Highlight the challenges, joys, and emotions of his journey. • Example 2: Clara's Story and the Love for Unique Flavors • Present Clara's story, who opened a gelateria focused on unique flavors inspired by local traditions. Describe how her emotional connection to flavors influenced the success of her business.

1.2 Detailed Overview: •

Case Study: "Dolcezza Italiana" Gelateria in Florence • Explore the "Dolcezza Italiana" gelateria and how the founder structured their entrepreneurial journey. Analyze how they managed the transition from initial dreams to practical realization. • Curiosity Example: The Mobile Gelateria that Conquered the City • Present an intriguing example of a mobile gelateria that captured the community's attention, arousing readers' curiosity.

1.3 Importance of the Art of Gelato: •

Tradition Example: "Sapori Antichi" Gelateria in Sicily • Deepen the connection between the art of gelato and local traditions, using the "Sapori Antichi" gelateria in Sicily as an example of artisanal excellence. • Unique Experience Example: "Gusto Magico" Gelateria in Rome • Illustrate how the art of gelato can create a unique experience by exploring the "Gusto Magico" gelateria and its ability to create innovative flavors.

1.4 Captivating Personal Reflections: •

Structured Reflection Guide: Your Vision of the Perfect Gelateria • Provide a structured guide for personal reflections, encouraging the reader to explore their vision of an ideal gelateria. • Empathy Invitation: Put Yourself in the Shoes of a Gelato Maker • Encourage empathy by inviting readers to imagine themselves at the helm of a gelateria and reflect on the emotions involved.

The inclusion of examples and case studies will make the chapter more engaging, offering readers concrete inspirations drawn from real experiences.

Chapter 2: Dreams and Aspirations - Development

Introduction: The Journey of the Aspiring Gelato Maker

The second chapter of this journey dedicated to the art of gelato focuses on the dreams and aspirations of those who wish to embark on the fascinating path of becoming gelato makers. This chapter serves as an empathetic and inspiring guide, providing in-depth analysis of the key elements that make up the landscape of entrepreneurial dreams in the world of artisanal gelato.

1. **Identification of Passion:** The First Step Towards the Dream

- Recognizing Passion: The chapter begins with a reflection on the process of recognizing and accepting the passion for gelato. Through engaging narratives, it explores how to identify personal passion and how it becomes the driving force for every aspiring gelato maker.

- **The Role of Dreams:** Dreams are examined as catalysts that fuel passion, providing the energy needed to embark on the journey to establish a business in the world of gelato.

2. Risks and Rewards: Facing the Challenges of the Journey

- **Risk Assessment:** Through case studies and testimonials, the challenges and risks associated with deviating from more conventional paths to pursue a career in artisanal gelato are explored.

- **Emotional and Professional Rewards:** The chapter highlights the emotional and professional rewards that come from following one's passion, offering a balanced perspective between the obstacles and joys of the journey.

3. Continuous Learning: The Key to Excellence

- **Training Courses and Self-Learning:** The importance of continuous learning in the field of gelato making is emphasized. Different training opportunities, including specialized courses and self-learning, are explored as fundamental elements for acquiring key skills.

- **Experimentation and Innovation:** The chapter encourages experimentation and innovation as essential tools to keep the passion alive and adapt to new industry trends.

4. Transformation of Passion into Entrepreneurial Skills

- **From Connoisseur to Producer:** Through practical examples, the chapter explores the transformation of the passion for gelato into solid entrepreneurial skills. It analyzes the practical steps to transition from a mere connoisseur to a successful gelato producer.

- **Market Research and Adaptability:** The importance of market research and the ability to adapt to the public's needs are emphasized, outlining strategies to maintain relevance in the market.

Conclusion: The Journey Toward Dream Realization The chapter concludes by offering a balanced and realistic perspective on the path from a passion for gelato to its realization in a successful business. Through anecdotes, practical advice, and a step-by-step guide, the reader is guided in transforming dreams into an entrepreneurial reality in the world of artisanal gelato.

Strengths and Areas for Improvement: Chapter 2

Chapter 2: Dreams and Aspirations - Evaluation

Strengths:

1. **Empathy and Reader Engagement:** •

   Strength: Engaging and empathetic narration conveys a personal connection with the dreams and aspirations of aspiring gelato makers.

2. **Psychological Depth:** •

Strength: In-depth analysis of the role of dreams and passion offers a profound psychological understanding, contributing to establishing an emotional bond with the reader.

3. **Balance Between Challenges and Rewards:** •

4. Strength: The balanced presentation of challenges and rewards provides a realistic view of the entrepreneurial journey in the gelato industry.

5. Practical Advice: • Strength: Inclusion of practical advice, such as the importance of continuous learning and experimentation, offers readers concrete guidance to pursue their dreams.

Areas for Improvement:

1. **In-depth Analysis of Risks and Management Strategies:** •

   Area for Improvement: Further expand the analysis of associated risks, providing specific management strategies to address entrepreneurial challenges.

2. **Diversification of Examples:** •

   Area for Improvement: Integrate greater diversity in examples and case studies, covering a broader range of entrepreneurial paths in the gelato industry.

3. **Deepening the Discussion on Market Adaptability:** •

4. **Area for Improvement:**

   Expand the discussion on market adaptability, including specific strategies to remain relevant in the evolving dynamics of the industry.

5. **Active Reader Involvement:** •

   Area for Improvement: Incorporate interactive elements or practical exercises to actively engage the reader in reflection and application of presented concepts.

Conclusions: The chapter on aspirations and dreams has a solid foundation, with compelling storytelling and practical advice. Expansion on specific areas and a greater variety of examples could further enhance its effectiveness in inspiring and guiding readers on their journey into the fascinating world of artisanal gelato.

Weaknesses and Errors to Avoid: Chapter 2

Chapter 2: Dreams and Aspirations - Weaknesses and Errors to Avoid

Weaknesses:

1. **Limited Examples:** •

Weakness: The limited number of examples may reduce the variety of experiences presented, making the chapter less inclusive for a diverse audience.

2. **Excessively Psychological Details:** •

Weakness: The psychological depth may be too dense for some readers, risking losing the attention of those seeking a more practical guide.

3. **Lack of Diversification in Challenges:** •

Weakness: The lack of diversification in discussed challenges may not cover a wide range of entrepreneurial scenarios, limiting the relevance of the chapter.

4. **Absence of Stress Elaboration:** •

Weakness: The absence of an elaboration on the stress associated with pursuing entrepreneurial dreams might underestimate a significant component of the journey.

Errors to Avoid:

1. **Excessive Generalizations:** •

Error to Avoid: Avoiding excessive generalizations can ensure that the chapter remains grounded in reality, preventing the portrayal of an overly idealized image of the entrepreneurial path.

2. **Lack of Practical Solutions:** •

Error to Avoid: Not providing practical solutions to address presented challenges may leave readers without a clear guide on overcoming obstacles.

3. **Lack of Cultural References:** •

Error to Avoid: Not including cultural references may limit the accessibility of the chapter, making it less relevant to readers from different backgrounds.

4. **Ignoring Economic Context:** •

Error to Avoid: Ignoring the economic context may make the chapter less adaptable to periods of economic uncertainty, neglecting the need to consider external factors.

Conclusions: Despite the chapter's solidity, expanding on a variety of entrepreneurial experiences, providing more practical solutions, and adapting to cultural diversities could enhance its effectiveness and relevance for a broader audience. Avoiding excessive generalizations and ensuring a grounding in the everyday entrepreneurial reality are essential elements to maintain the chapter's credibility.

Examples and Case Studies: Chapter 2

Chapter 2: Dreams and Aspirations - Examples and Case Studies

Case Study 1: "Sofia's Journey: From Passion to Artisanal Gelateria" Background: Sofia, a former marketing professional, always harbored a secret passion for creating artisanal sweets. After attending gelato courses and experimenting in the kitchen, she opened her artisanal gelateria in the heart of the city. Key Aspects: • Passion as a Guide: Sofia identified her passion for creating gelato as the main driver for her career change. • Training and Experimentation: She invested time in training, attending specific courses, and continuously experimenting to develop unique flavors. • Faced Risks: Transitioning from a established career to the gelato industry posed a significant risk, but Sofia faced the challenge with determination.

Example 1: "Marco's Dream - Gelato that Tells Stories" Background: Marco, a young aspiring gelato maker, nurtured the dream of creating gelato that tells stories. He opened a gelateria focusing on the narration behind each flavor, tying each gelato to a unique story. Key Aspects: • Creativity and Innovation: Marco brought innovation through creativity, developing flavors inspired by personal

Chapter 3: The Perfect Flavor - Development

Introduction: The Art of Creating the Ideal Flavor

The third chapter of this exploration into the world of artisanal ice cream focuses on the central element of this craft: the perfect flavor. In this chapter, we will delve into the intricacies of creating flavors that captivate the imagination, satisfy the senses, and define excellence in the world of ice cream.

1. **The Science of Flavor Balancing:**
   - Flavor Depth: We will begin by exploring the science behind flavor balancing, understanding how the harmony between sweetness, acidity, bitterness, and creaminess contributes to defining the depth of an ice cream.
   - Ingredient Utilization: We will examine the importance of selecting high-quality ingredients and their combination to create synergies that elevate the overall taste of the ice cream.
2. **Creativity in Flavors and Bold Combinations:**
   - Creative Experimentation: Encouraging creative experimentation, we will explore how innovative gelato makers have brought new perspectives to the traditional world of ice cream flavors.
   - Unusual and Refined Combinations: We will examine case studies of ice cream parlors that have embraced unusual and refined combinations, taking readers on a unique sensory journey.

3.	**From Creation to Presentation:**
- 	Art of Presentation: We will delve into the art of presenting ice cream, exploring how the visual aspect influences the customer's perception of taste.
- 	Innovative Technologies: Including a discussion on innovative technologies used in the creation and presentation process, such as the use of 3D printers for intricate shapes.
4.	Community Engagement and Customer Feedback:
- 	Tasting Events and Engagement: Exploring how actively engaging the community through tasting events and meetings with gelato makers can influence the creation of new flavors.
- 	Importance of Customer Feedback: Analyzing the importance of customer feedback in perfecting flavors, opening a dialogue between gelato makers and consumers.

Conclusion: The Perfect Flavor as a Complete Experience

The chapter will conclude by emphasizing how the creation of the perfect flavor goes beyond the mere combination of ingredients. It involves passion, creativity, and the ability to interpret the desires of consumers. Through examples, case studies, and practical advice, readers will be guided to explore the art of creating ice cream that goes beyond simple taste, becoming an unforgettable multisensory experience.

Strengths and Areas for Improvement: Chapter 3: The Perfect Flavor

Chapter 3: The Perfect Flavor - Evaluation

Strengths:

1.	**Scientific Depth:**
- 	Strength: The scientific depth on flavor balancing provides a solid foundation, making the chapter informative and accessible even to readers with a technical interest.
2.	**Creativity and Innovation:**
- 	Strength: The focus on creativity and innovation in flavor combinations demonstrates how the gelateria can be an evolving artistic field.
3.	**Community Engagement:**
- 	Strength: The inclusion of community engagement and customer feedback adds a practical and relational element, connecting the creative process to consumer satisfaction.
4.	**Multisensory Approach:**
- 	Strength: Emphasizing the visual aspect and multisensory experience of taste highlights the importance of engaging all senses in the ice cream creation process.

Areas for Improvement:

1. **Diversification of Case Studies:**
   - Area for Improvement: Expanding the diversification of case studies could further enrich the reader's experience, offering a more comprehensive view of the diverse realities of gelateria.
2. **In-depth Exploration of Innovative Techniques:**
   - Area for Improvement: Greater exploration of innovative techniques could provide readers with a more detailed overview of how technology can influence ice cream creation and presentation.
3. **Inclusion of Practical Exercises:**
   - Area for Improvement: The inclusion of practical exercises could actively engage the reader, providing opportunities to directly apply the concepts learned.
4. **Market Trend Analysis:**
   - Area for Improvement: Adding a section that analyzes market trends could help readers understand how consumer preferences influence flavor creation.

Conclusion:

The chapter on creating the Perfect Flavor has a solid foundation, but expanding on specific topics and greater diversification in case studies could make it even more engaging for a broad audience. Integrating practical exercises can facilitate a more direct application of concepts, ensuring readers can translate theory into practice in the world of artisanal ice cream.

Weaknesses and Errors to Avoid: Chapter 3: The Perfect Flavor

Chapter 3: The Perfect Flavor - Weaknesses and Errors to Avoid

Weaknesses:

1. **Overly Complex Scientific Details:**
   - Weakness: The scientific depth may be too complex for non-expert readers, risking losing the interest of those seeking a more accessible understanding.
2. **Limited Focus on Traditional Flavors:**
   - Weakness: The focus on innovative flavor combinations might overlook the importance of traditional flavors, limiting the completeness of the discussion.
3. **Lack of Depth on Presentation Techniques:**
   - Weakness: The lack of depth on presentation techniques might overlook a key aspect, considering how the visual aspect influences taste perception.
4. **Limitations in Discussing Innovative Techniques:**
   - Weakness: The discussion on innovative techniques may be limited, depriving the reader of a comprehensive understanding of the opportunities offered by technology in the field of gelateria.

Errors to Avoid:

1.   **Idealization of the Creative Process:**
    - Error to Avoid: Avoiding excessive idealization of the creative process can ensure that the reader has a realistic view of the challenges and complexities involved in creating the perfect flavor.
2.   **Lack of Market References:**
    - Error to Avoid: Ignoring market references could deprive the reader of an understanding of business dynamics and consumer preferences that can influence flavor creation.
3.   **Lack of Practical Advice:**
    - Error to Avoid: Not providing practical advice could limit the applicability of the chapter in the reader's daily life, making the content less immediately useful.
4.   **Ignoring the Diversity of Audience Tastes:**
    - Error to Avoid: Ignoring the diversity of audience tastes could lead to a too creator-centric view, neglecting the importance of adapting to consumer preferences.

Conclusion:

To improve the chapter on creating the Perfect Flavor, it is essential to simplify complex scientific concepts, expand the discussion of innovative techniques, and ensure a balanced view between tradition and innovation. Avoiding excessive idealization and providing practical advice will make the chapter more accessible and applicable in the realm of artisanal ice cream.

Examples and Case Studies: Chapter 3: The Perfect Flavor

Chapter 3: The Perfect Flavor - Examples and Case Studies

Case Study 1: "Carla's Innovation - Seasonally Inspired Flavors"

Background: Carla, a passionate gelato maker, revolutionized her lab by introducing seasonally inspired flavors. During the summer, she offers fresh gelatos with seasonal fruit, while in winter, she creates warm sorbets with winter flavors.

Key Aspects:

- Seasonal Creativity: Carla demonstrated how seasonal creativity can positively influence the customer experience, adapting flavors to seasonal preferences and expectations. Community Involvement:
- Actively engaged the community in selecting seasonal flavors, organizing participatory tastings, and online surveys.

Example 1: "Marco's Territory Flavors - Valuing Local Excellences"

Background: Marco, an enthusiastic gelato maker, focused his production on local flavors. He uses ingredients from local producers, creating gelatos that tell the story of the region.

Key Aspects:

- Valorizing Local Excellences: Marco showed how valuing local excellences can create a deeper connection with the community, emphasizing the importance of supporting local producers. Stories Behind the Flavors:
- Each flavor is accompanied by a story that narrates the origin of the ingredients, involving customers in a sensory and cultural journey.

Case Study 2: "Alessio's 3D Ice Creams - Creating Artistic Taste Experiences"

Background: Alessio introduced a new dimension to the art of ice cream presentation by creating 3D artworks using food printers. In addition to taste, his ice creams are appreciated for their unique visual appeal.

Key Aspects:

- Innovation in Presentation: Alessio demonstrated how innovation in presentation can capture customer attention, transforming ice cream creation into a comprehensive form of art. Social Media Engagement:
- Engaged the community through social media, sharing videos of the creative process and encouraging customers to share their experiences online.

Example 2: "Maria's Intercultural Flavors - Fusions of Tastes from Around the World"

Background: Maria brought her passion for travel into creating intercultural flavors, blending tastes from different parts of the world. She offers gelatos that represent a fusion of culinary traditions.

Key Aspects:

- Exploration of Cultures: Maria showed how exploring and respecting diverse cultures can enrich the range of flavors, providing a global perspective through ice cream. Themed Events:
- Organizes themed events where she introduces new flavors inspired by a specific culture, engaging the community in discovering new tastes.

These examples and case studies highlight the wide variety of approaches possible in creating the perfect flavor. From seasonal innovations to valuing local excellences, from artistic presentation to intercultural fusion, each gelato maker has a unique story to tell through their flavors.

Chapter 4: Store Design - Development

Introduction: Creating a Welcoming and Memorable Environment

The fourth chapter focuses on a fundamental aspect of artisanal gelato shops: store design. Creating a welcoming and memorable environment not only enhances the customer experience but also reflects the unique identity of the gelateria.

1. **Conception of Atmosphere:**

   - Store Style and Theme: Explore how the style and theme of the store can influence the atmosphere, creating a visual identity that aligns with the values and personality of the gelateria.

   - Use of Colors and Materials: Analyze the importance of strategically using colors and materials, considering how they can influence the emotions of customers.

2. **Strategic Layout and Customer Flow:**

   - Organization of Spaces: Examine how to organize internal spaces, optimizing the layout for a smooth customer flow and effective product presentation.

   - Focal Points: Introduce the idea of focal points, strategically positioning key products to capture attention and stimulate appetite.

3. **Creation of Experiential Zones:**

   - Open Production Area: Explore the positive effect of an open production area where customers can observe the gelato-making process, creating an interactive experience.

   - Relaxation and Socialization Areas: Consider the importance of relaxation and socialization areas, transforming the gelateria into a community gathering space.

4. **Elements of Creative and Innovative Design:**

   - Artistic Installations and Themed Displays: Examine how artistic installations and themed displays can add a creative touch to store design, making it unique and memorable.

   - Use of Interactive Technologies: Introduce the idea of using interactive technologies, such as digital screens or mobile apps, to engage customers and enhance the overall experience.

5. **Practical and Sustainable Considerations:**

- Energy Efficiency and Sustainable Materials: Explore the importance of energy efficiency and the use of sustainable materials, reflecting the growing attention to eco-friendly business practices.

- Universal Accessibility: Consider universal accessibility, ensuring that store design is open and welcoming to all customers, regardless of their needs.

Conclusion: Transforming the Store into a Unique Experience

The chapter will conclude by emphasizing that store design is not just an aesthetic matter but an essential component in offering a unique experience. Through examples, case studies, and practical tips, readers will be guided in creating an environment that reflects the gelateria's personality and leaves a lasting impression on customers.

Strengths and Areas for Improvement: Chapter 4: Store Design

Chapter 4: Store Design - Evaluation

Strengths:

1. **Multisensory Approach:**

   - Strength: The multisensory approach in considering colors, materials, and atmosphere contributes to creating an engaging experience for customers.

2. **Focus on Customer Flow:**

   - Strength: The focus on strategic layout and customer flow highlights the practicality of design, ensuring smooth navigation and effective product presentation.

3. **Creative and Innovative Elements:**

   - Strength: The introduction of creative elements, such as artistic installations and interactive technologies, contributes to making the store unique and memorable.

4. **Sustainability and Accessibility:**

   - Strength: Attention to sustainability and universal accessibility demonstrates a contemporary sensitivity to community needs and environmental concerns.

Areas for Improvement:

1. **Practical Details:**

   - Area for Improvement: Including practical details, such as specific advice on furniture arrangement, could make the chapter even more applicable in the daily practice of gelato makers.

2. **Diversification of Case Studies:**

- Area for Improvement: Expanding the diversification of case studies by including examples of stores of different sizes and cultural environments could provide a more comprehensive picture of design possibilities.

3. **In-depth Exploration of Interactive Technologies:**

   - Area for Improvement: A specific in-depth exploration of interactive technologies could be useful, offering practical details on how to successfully implement them in the context of a gelateria.

4. **Advice on Brand Incorporation:**

   - Area for Improvement: Adding practical advice on incorporating the brand into design, ensuring visual consistency that reflects the gelateria's identity.

Conclusion:

The chapter on store design has solid strengths, but the addition of practical details, greater diversification in case studies, and specific insights into certain topics could make the content even more comprehensive and usable for those looking to enhance the physical aspect of their gelateria.

Weaknesses and Errors to Avoid: Chapter 4: Store Design

Chapter 4: Store Design - Weaknesses and Errors to Avoid

Weaknesses:

1. **Lack of Practical Details:**

   - Weakness: The lack of practical details, such as specific advice on furniture arrangement, could limit the applicability of the chapter in the daily practice of gelato makers.

2. **Limited Focus on Store Sizes and Types:**

   - Weakness: The focus on a generic approach might not consider specific sizes and types of stores, missing the opportunity to provide more targeted advice.

3. **Lack of Depth on Interactive Technologies:**

   - Weakness: The lack of specific depth on how to incorporate interactive technologies may make it challenging for gelato makers to implement such elements effectively.

Errors to Avoid:

1. **Copying Without Personalization:**

- Error to Avoid: Directly copying successful designs without personalization could lead to a lack of originality, not reflecting the uniqueness and identity of the gelateria.

2. **Ignoring Practical Aspects:**

   - Error to Avoid: Ignoring the practical aspect of design could result in aesthetic choices that compromise operational efficiency and convenience for customers.

3. **Underestimating the Importance of Accessibility:**

   - Error to Avoid: Underestimating the importance of accessibility could exclude a significant portion of the clientele, limiting the long-term success of the gelateria.

Conclusion:

To improve the chapter on store design, it is essential to integrate practical details and targeted advice, considering the diverse sizes and types of gelaterie. Avoiding the direct copying of others' designs and emphasizing the importance of accessibility will contribute to a more balanced and sustainable approach in creating welcoming and memorable environments.

Examples and Case Studies: Chapter 4: Store Design

Chapter 4: Store Design - Examples and Case Studies

Case Study 1: "Luca's Vintage Gelato - Retro Atmosphere and Warm Welcome" Background: Luca has created a gelateria with a design that evokes vintage charm. The use of vintage furniture, warm colors, and soft lighting creates a welcoming and familial atmosphere. Key Aspects:

- Stylistic Consistency: Luca has demonstrated how stylistic consistency, in his case, vintage, can create a distinctive atmosphere that is also reflected in the products offered.

- Community Engagement: Organizes vintage-themed events, involving the community in a reenactment of past traditions.

Example 1: "Sofia's Minimalism - Simplicity that Inspires Elegance" Background: Sofia has adopted a minimalist approach to her store's design. With white walls, clean lines, and essential furnishings, she has created an environment that inspires elegance and sophistication. Key Aspects:

- Impact of Simplicity: Sofia has shown how simplicity can be highly effective, focusing attention on products and creating a tranquil atmosphere.

- Sensory Experiences: Uses light fragrances and soft music to enrich the sensory experience, demonstrating how even minimal design can engage the senses.

Case Study 2: "Marco's Technological Innovation - Gelateria 4.0" Background: Marco has integrated interactive technologies into his store's design. Digital screens allow customers to customize their ice cream, creating a unique and engaging experience. Key Aspects:

- Interactivity: Marco has demonstrated how interactivity can be used to engage customers, offering them an active role in creating their own product.

- Online Promotion: Uses technological experiences for online promotion, encouraging customers to share their creations on social media.

Example 2: "Marta's Eco-friendly Gelato - Sustainable Design" Background: Marta has designed her gelateria with a strong focus on sustainability. Recycled materials, energy-efficient lighting, and a green wall create an eco-friendly environment. Key Aspects:

- Environmental Responsibility: Marta has shown how environmental attention can not only reduce ecological impact but also attract customers sensitive to environmental concerns.

- Community Involvement: Organizes environmental cleanup events and promotes local sustainability initiatives, involving the community in the store's eco-friendly mission.

These examples and case studies highlight how store design can be adapted to different themes and goals. From vintage atmosphere to minimalist simplicity, from technological innovation to sustainability, each approach has the potential to create a unique and engaging environment

Chapter 5: Taste Marketing - Development

Introduction: Communicating the Taste Experience

The fifth chapter focuses on taste marketing, a crucial aspect for attracting customers and creating a successful brand. The ability to effectively communicate the taste experience is fundamental to differentiate oneself in the artisanal gelato market.

1. **Creating an Engaging Taste Narrative:**

    - Taste Descriptions: Explore how to describe tastes in an engaging way, using language that stimulates imagination and arouses desire in customers.

    - Stories Behind the Products: Introduce the idea of telling compelling stories behind products, connecting tastes to unique experiences, traditions, or inspirations.

2. **Effective Use of Social Media:**

- Gastronomic Photography: Examine the importance of gastronomic photography, showing how captivating images of products can generate interest and desire.
- Community Engagement: Introduce strategies to engage the community on social media, encouraging the sharing of experiences and opinions related to the offered tastes.

3. **Tasting Events and Collaborations:**

- Themed Events: Explore how to organize themed events or tastings, offering customers the opportunity to explore new tastes and create a memorable experience.
- Collaborations with Other Brands: Introduce the possibility of collaborations with other brands or local companies, expanding the marketing reach through strategic synergies.

4. **Loyalty Programs and Special Offers:**

- Personalized Loyalty Programs: Examine the effectiveness of personalized loyalty programs, focusing on customers' favorite tastes and offering special deals on new creations.
- Limited-Time Offers: Introduce the idea of limited-time offers, creating a sense of urgency and stimulating the trial of new tastes.

5. **Experiential Marketing:**

- Engagement of the Senses: Explore how to engage the senses through marketing, using strategies that go beyond textual description to create a multisensory experience.
- Creating Unique Taste Events: Introduce the possibility of creating unique taste events, such as themed nights or workshops, to engage the community in immersive experiences.

Conclusion: Creating Desire through Taste Marketing

The chapter will conclude by emphasizing how taste marketing goes beyond simple advertising, seeking to create desire and emotional connection between customers and the offered products. Through innovative and engaging strategies, gelato makers can transform taste communication into a distinctive competitive advantage.

Strengths and Areas for Improvement: Chapter 5: Taste Marketing

Chapter 5: Taste Marketing - Evaluation

Strengths:

1. **Engaging Taste Narrative:**
   - Strength: The engaging taste narrative represents a strong point, creating an emotional bond between customers and products, stimulating the desire to experience new tastes.

2. **Effective Use of Social Media:**
   - Strength: The approach to social media marketing, especially the use of gastronomic photography, is effective in capturing customers' attention and generating interest.

3. **Tasting Events and Collaborations:**
   - Strength: The organization of themed events and collaborations with other brands offers an opportunity for direct customer engagement, expanding brand visibility.

4. **Loyalty Programs and Special Offers:**
   - Strength: The implementation of personalized loyalty programs and limited-time offers is a strength that encourages customer loyalty and stimulates the trial of new tastes.

5. **Experiential Marketing:**
   - Strength: The engagement of the senses and the creation of unique taste events contribute to transforming marketing into a multisensory experience, making the brand more memorable.

Areas for Improvement:

1. **In-depth Exploration of Gastronomic Photography:**
   - Area for Improvement: A deeper exploration of gastronomic photography, with practical tips and specific advice, could further enhance the effectiveness of the chapter.

2. **Expansion of Case Studies:**
   - Area for Improvement: Adding more case studies, including examples of taste marketing in different cultural contexts, could enrich readers' understanding.

3. **Practical Advice for Events and Collaborations:**
   - Area for Improvement: Integrating practical advice on how to organize tasting events and manage collaborations can make the chapter even more useful for gelato makers.

4. **In-depth Exploration of Social Media Engagement Techniques:**

- Area for Improvement: A more in-depth exploration of specific techniques for engaging the community on social media could offer a more detailed guide.

5. **Considerations on Budget and Resources:**

- Area for Improvement: Adding practical considerations on the budget and resources needed to successfully implement the proposed marketing strategies.

Conclusion:

The chapter on taste marketing has solid strengths, but the addition of specific details, practical advice, and an in-depth exploration of some topics can further improve its utility for gelato makers looking to enhance the promotion of their products.

Weaknesses and Errors to Avoid: Chapter 5: Taste Marketing

Chapter 5: Taste Marketing - Weaknesses and Errors to Avoid

Weaknesses:

1. **Gastronomic Photography:**

- Weakness: The section on gastronomic photography might be too superficial. A more in-depth exploration with practical examples and specific techniques would have been useful.

2. **Practical Advice for Events and Collaborations:**

- Weakness: The lack of specific practical advice on how to organize tasting events and manage collaborations could make the proposed strategies less accessible for gelato makers.

3. **Social Media Engagement Techniques:**

- Weakness: The section on social media engagement could have benefited from a more detailed exploration of specific techniques for generating interaction and participation.

Errors to Avoid:

1. **Ignoring the Specificity of the Target Audience:**

- Error to Avoid: Ignoring the specificity of the target audience could lead to ineffective marketing strategies. Adapting campaigns to the tastes and preferences of the audience is crucial.

2. **Neglecting Results Analysis:**

- Error to Avoid: Neglecting the analysis of results from marketing campaigns can hinder learning and adaptation. Monitoring metrics is crucial for continuous improvement.

3. **Lack of Consistency in the Narrative:**

   - Error to Avoid: Lack of consistency in the narrative can confuse customers. Maintaining a clear and recognizable story contributes to consolidating the brand's identity.

Conclusion:

The chapter presents weaknesses in the depth of some sections and the lack of specific practical advice. Avoiding errors such as ignoring the specificity of the target audience or neglecting results analysis is crucial for effective taste marketing. Integrating practical advice and specific details will contribute to improving the chapter's utility for gelato makers.

Examples and Case Studies: Chapter 5: Taste Marketing

Chapter 5: Taste Marketing - Examples and Case Studies

Case Study 1: "Gelateria da Maria's Exclusive Taste Campaign" Background: Gelateria da Maria launched an exclusive taste campaign, creating a new flavor every month available only for a limited period. This created a sense of urgency and anticipation among customers. Key Aspects:

- Time Limitation: The time limitation of the taste stimulated immediate trial and generated strong online interaction, with customers sharing their experiences on social media. Community Engagement:

- The gelateria involved the community in choosing monthly flavors through online surveys, creating a sense of participation and inclusion.

Example 1: "GelatoArt's Instagram Strategy" Background: GelatoArt implemented an Instagram strategy that goes beyond simply posting pictures of products. They created daily behind-the-scenes stories, showing the creative process behind each flavor and engaging the community. Key Aspects:

- Engaging Stories: Daily stories added a narrative element, allowing customers to emotionally connect with the brand and its products. Active Participation:

- GelatoArt encouraged active customer participation, asking them to share their favorite tastes and suggestions for new creations through specific hashtags.

Case Study 2: "Gelateria del Cuore's Taste Festival" Background: Gelateria del Cuore organized an annual "Taste Festival" where they showcased a selection of unique and limited flavors over a week. The festival became an anticipated event in the community. Key Aspects:

- Unique Experience: The festival offered a unique experience, encouraging customers to try a variety of flavors in a short period. Community Involvement:

- The gelateria involved the community in planning the festival, seeking suggestions for new tastes and organizing online voting for the final selection.

Example 2: "Gelateria Insieme's Unique Taste Collaboration" Background: Gelateria Insieme collaborated with local restaurants to create unique flavors inspired by iconic local dishes. This collaboration offered an innovative culinary perspective and sparked curiosity among customers. Key Aspects:

- Synergy with Local Cuisine: The collaboration created synergy with local cuisine, offering customers an experience beyond traditional gelato. Cross-Promotion:

- The gelateria implemented cross-promotion strategies with the involved restaurants, expanding the visibility of the campaign and attracting new customers.

These examples and case studies demonstrate how innovative and engaging taste marketing strategies can help differentiate a gelateria in the market, creating a deeper connection with the community and stimulating customers' curiosity.

Future: Chapter 5: Taste Marketing

Chapter 5: Taste Marketing - Looking to the Future

1. **Integration of Augmented Reality (AR):**

   - Virtual Taste Experiences: With the advancement of AR technology, gelaterias could offer virtual taste experiences, allowing customers to "taste" flavors through digital devices before making a purchase.

   - Virtual Customization: The ability to virtually customize one's gelato could become a trend, allowing customers to interactively experience flavor combinations.

2. **Sustainable Marketing Strategies:**

   - Sustainability as a Key Focus: Gelaterias might focus more on sustainability as a key point in taste marketing, communicating eco-friendly practices in production and promoting flavors with low environmental impact.

   - Community Involvement: Collaborating with local sustainable initiatives could become a central element, involving the community in shared actions for environmental conservation.

3. **Advanced Multisensory Experiences:**

- Sensory Engagement: The evolution of technologies could enable advanced multisensory experiences, engaging not only sight and taste but also hearing and touch through innovative devices.

- Interactive Sensory Events: Gelaterias could organize interactive sensory events where customers can experience the creation of flavors in new and engaging ways.

4. **Empathetic Marketing:**

- Stories Behind the Products: The future of taste marketing could embrace an even more empathetic narrative, telling stories behind the products that not only emotionally engage customers but also connect to social or humanitarian causes.

- Sensitivity to Customer Needs: Marketing strategies could be more sensitive to the specific needs of customers, personalizing not only tastes but also stories and campaigns based on individual preferences and values.

5. **Blockchain Technologies for Ingredient Traceability:**

- Quality and Origin Assurance: Implementing blockchain technologies could ensure greater traceability of ingredients, providing customers with certainty about the quality and origin of elements used in the proposed flavors.

- Consumer Involvement: Involving consumers in the origin story of ingredients could become a distinctive strategy in taste marketing.

Conclusion:

Looking to the future, innovation in taste marketing relies on the integration of advanced technologies, attention to sustainability, and deepening emotional connections with customers. The continuous evolution of the industry will offer increasingly creative opportunities to distinguish gelaterias in the market and create unique taste experiences

Chapter 5: Taste Marketing - Development

Introduction: Communicating the Taste Experience

The fifth chapter focuses on taste marketing, a crucial aspect for attracting customers and creating a successful brand. The ability to effectively communicate the taste experience is fundamental to differentiate oneself in the artisanal gelato market.

1. **Creating an Engaging Taste Narrative:**

- Taste Descriptions: Explore how to describe tastes in an engaging way, using language that stimulates imagination and arouses desire in customers.

- Stories Behind the Products: Introduce the idea of telling compelling stories behind products, connecting tastes to unique experiences, traditions, or inspirations.

2. **Effective Use of Social Media:**

- Gastronomic Photography: Examine the importance of gastronomic photography, showing how captivating images of products can generate interest and desire.

- Community Engagement: Introduce strategies to engage the community on social media, encouraging the sharing of experiences and opinions related to the offered tastes.

3. **Tasting Events and Collaborations:**

- Themed Events: Explore how to organize themed events or tastings, offering customers the opportunity to explore new tastes and create a memorable experience.

- Collaborations with Other Brands: Introduce the possibility of collaborations with other brands or local companies, expanding the marketing reach through strategic synergies.

4. **Loyalty Programs and Special Offers:**

- Personalized Loyalty Programs: Examine the effectiveness of personalized loyalty programs, focusing on customers' favorite tastes and offering special deals on new creations.

- Limited-Time Offers: Introduce the idea of limited-time offers, creating a sense of urgency and stimulating the trial of new tastes.

5. **Experiential Marketing:**

- Engagement of the Senses: Explore how to engage the senses through marketing, using strategies that go beyond textual description to create a multisensory experience.

- Creating Unique Taste Events: Introduce the possibility of creating unique taste events, such as themed nights or workshops, to engage the community in immersive experiences.

Conclusion: Creating Desire through Taste Marketing

The chapter will conclude by emphasizing how taste marketing goes beyond simple advertising, seeking to create desire and emotional connection between customers and the offered products.

Through innovative and engaging strategies, gelato makers can transform taste communication into a distinctive competitive advantage.

Strengths and Areas for Improvement: Chapter 5: Taste Marketing

Chapter 5: Taste Marketing - Evaluation

Strengths:

1. **Engaging Taste Narrative:**

   - Strength: The engaging taste narrative represents a strong point, creating an emotional bond between customers and products, stimulating the desire to experience new tastes.

2. **Effective Use of Social Media:**

   - Strength: The approach to social media marketing, especially the use of gastronomic photography, is effective in capturing customers' attention and generating interest.

3. **Tasting Events and Collaborations:**

   - Strength: The organization of themed events and collaborations with other brands offers an opportunity for direct customer engagement, expanding brand visibility.

4. **Loyalty Programs and Special Offers:**

   - Strength: The implementation of personalized loyalty programs and limited-time offers is a strength that encourages customer loyalty and stimulates the trial of new tastes.

5. **Experiential Marketing:**

   - Strength: The engagement of the senses and the creation of unique taste events contribute to transforming marketing into a multisensory experience, making the brand more memorable.

Areas for Improvement:

1. **In-depth Exploration of Gastronomic Photography:**

   - Area for Improvement: A deeper exploration of gastronomic photography, with practical tips and specific advice, could further enhance the effectiveness of the chapter.

2. **Expansion of Case Studies:**

   - Area for Improvement: Adding more case studies, including examples of taste marketing in different cultural contexts, could enrich readers' understanding.

3. **Practical Advice for Events and Collaborations:**

   - Area for Improvement: Integrating practical advice on how to organize tasting events and manage collaborations can make the chapter even more useful for gelato makers.

4. **In-depth Exploration of Social Media Engagement Techniques:**

   - Area for Improvement: A more in-depth exploration of specific techniques for engaging the community on social media could offer a more detailed guide.

5. **Considerations on Budget and Resources:**

   - **Area for Improvement: Adding practical considerations on the budget and resources needed to successfully implement the proposed marketing strategies.**

Conclusion:

The chapter on taste marketing has solid strengths, but the addition of specific details, practical advice, and an in-depth exploration of some topics can further improve its utility for gelato makers looking to enhance the promotion of their products.

Weaknesses and Errors to Avoid: Chapter 5: Taste Marketing

Chapter 5: Taste Marketing - Weaknesses and Errors to Avoid

Weaknesses:

1. **Gastronomic Photography:**

   - Weakness: The section on gastronomic photography might be too superficial. A more in-depth exploration with practical examples and specific techniques would have been useful.

2. **Practical Advice for Events and Collaborations:**

   - Weakness: The lack of specific practical advice on how to organize tasting events and manage collaborations could make the proposed strategies less accessible for gelato makers.

3. **Social Media Engagement Techniques:**

   - Weakness: The section on social media engagement could have benefited from a more detailed exploration of specific techniques for generating interaction and participation.

Errors to Avoid:

1. **Ignoring the Specificity of the Target Audience:**

- Error to Avoid: Ignoring the specificity of the target audience could lead to ineffective marketing strategies. Adapting campaigns to the tastes and preferences of the audience is crucial.

2. **Neglecting Results Analysis:**

- Error to Avoid: Neglecting the analysis of results from marketing campaigns can hinder learning and adaptation. Monitoring metrics is crucial for continuous improvement.

3. **Lack of Consistency in the Narrative:**

- Error to Avoid: Lack of consistency in the narrative can confuse customers. Maintaining a clear and recognizable story contributes to consolidating the brand's identity.

Conclusion:

The chapter presents weaknesses in the depth of some sections and the lack of specific practical advice. Avoiding errors such as ignoring the specificity of the target audience or neglecting results analysis is crucial for effective taste marketing. Integrating practical advice and specific details will contribute to improving the chapter's utility for gelato makers.

Examples and Case Studies: Chapter 5: Taste Marketing

Chapter 5: Taste Marketing - Examples and Case Studies

Case Study 1: "Gelateria da Maria's Exclusive Taste Campaign" Background: Gelateria da Maria launched an exclusive taste campaign, creating a new flavor every month available only for a limited period. This created a sense of urgency and anticipation among customers. Key Aspects:

- Time Limitation: The time limitation of the taste stimulated immediate trial and generated strong online interaction, with customers sharing their experiences on social media. Community Engagement:

- The gelateria involved the community in choosing monthly flavors through online surveys, creating a sense of participation and inclusion.

Example 1: "GelatoArt's Instagram Strategy" Background: GelatoArt implemented an Instagram strategy that goes beyond simply posting pictures of products. They created daily behind-the-scenes stories, showing the creative process behind each flavor and engaging the community. Key Aspects:

- Engaging Stories: Daily stories added a narrative element, allowing customers to emotionally connect with the brand and its products. Active Participation:

- GelatoArt encouraged active customer participation, asking them to share their favorite tastes and suggestions for new creations through specific hashtags.

Case Study 2: "Gelateria del Cuore's Taste Festival" Background: Gelateria del Cuore organized an annual "Taste Festival" where they showcased a selection of unique and limited flavors over a week. The festival became an anticipated event in the community. Key Aspects:

- Unique Experience: The festival offered a unique experience, encouraging customers to try a variety of flavors in a short period. Community Involvement:

- The gelateria involved the community in planning the festival, seeking suggestions for new tastes and organizing online voting for the final selection.

Example 2: "Gelateria Insieme's Unique Taste Collaboration" Background: Gelateria Insieme collaborated with local restaurants to create unique flavors inspired by iconic local dishes. This collaboration offered an innovative culinary perspective and sparked curiosity among customers. Key Aspects:

- Synergy with Local Cuisine: The collaboration created synergy with local cuisine, offering customers an experience beyond traditional gelato. Cross-Promotion:

- The gelateria implemented cross-promotion strategies with the involved restaurants, expanding the visibility of the campaign and attracting new customers.

These examples and case studies demonstrate how innovative and engaging taste marketing strategies can help differentiate a gelateria in the market, creating a deeper connection with the community and stimulating customers' curiosity.

Future: Chapter 5: Taste Marketing

Chapter 5: Taste Marketing - Looking to the Future

1. **Integration of Augmented Reality (AR):**

    - Virtual Taste Experiences: With the advancement of AR technology, gelaterias could offer virtual taste experiences, allowing customers to "taste" flavors through digital devices before making a purchase.

    - Virtual Customization: The ability to virtually customize one's gelato could become a trend, allowing customers to interactively experience flavor combinations.

2. **Sustainable Marketing Strategies:**

    - Sustainability as a Key Focus: Gelaterias might focus more on sustainability as a key point in taste marketing, communicating eco-friendly practices in production and promoting flavors with low environmental impact.

    - Community Involvement: Collaborating with local sustainable initiatives could become a central element, involving the community in shared actions for environmental conservation.

3. **Advanced Multisensory Experiences:**

- Sensory Engagement: The evolution of technologies could enable advanced multisensory experiences, engaging not only sight and taste but also hearing and touch through innovative devices.

- Interactive Sensory Events: Gelaterias could organize interactive sensory events where customers can experience the creation of flavors in new and engaging ways.

4. **Empathetic Marketing:**

- Stories Behind the Products: The future of taste marketing could embrace an even more empathetic narrative, telling stories behind the products that not only emotionally engage customers but also connect to social or humanitarian causes.

- Sensitivity to Customer Needs: Marketing strategies could be more sensitive to the specific needs of customers, personalizing not only tastes but also stories and campaigns based on individual preferences and values.

5. **Blockchain Technologies for Ingredient Traceability:**

- Quality and Origin Assurance: Implementing blockchain technologies could ensure greater traceability of ingredients, providing customers with certainty about the quality and origin of elements used in the proposed flavors.

- Consumer Involvement: Involving consumers in the origin story of ingredients could become a distinctive strategy in taste marketing.

Conclusion:

Looking to the future, innovation in taste marketing relies on the integration of advanced technologies, attention to sustainability, and deepening emotional connections with customers. The continuous evolution of the industry will offer increasingly creative opportunities to distinguish gelaterias in the market and create unique taste experiences.

Chapter 6: The Creative Process

Chapter 6: The Creative Process - Exploring the Art of Creating New Flavors

Introduction: The Magic Behind New Flavors

The sixth chapter delves into the fascinating world of the creative process behind the creation of new flavors. From initial inspiration to the final taste, we will explore the art and science that merge in producing unique and memorable gelatos.

1. **Inspiration and Ideation:**
   - Sources of Inspiration: Explore various sources of inspiration, ranging from travels and cultural traditions to seasonal or personal passions.
   - Creative Brainstorming: Introduce techniques for creative brainstorming to generate innovative ideas and stimulate the gelato maker's creativity.

2. **Ingredient Selection:**
   - Exploration of Ingredients: Practical guide on exploring new ingredients, from fresh fruits to exotic spices, to create unique taste profiles.
   - Balance and Harmony: How to balance ingredients to achieve harmony in flavors, avoiding excesses or unwanted subtleties.

3. **Experimentation and Recording:**
   - Creative Laboratory: Tips on organizing a creative laboratory to experiment with quantities and proportions, allowing gelato makers to refine recipes.
   - Record of Results: The importance of keeping a detailed record of results, noting variations and discoveries during the experimental process.

4. **Testing and Feedback:**
   - Tasting Panel: How to organize tasting sessions with an expert panel or simply involving loyal customers to obtain accurate feedback.
   - Adjustments and Refinements: The process of adapting based on received feedback to gradually perfect the new flavor.

5. **Presentation to the Public:**
   - Creating a Story Around the Flavor: Strategies for presenting the new flavor to the public, creating an engaging narrative connected to its creation.
   - Launch Events: How to organize launch events to generate interest and curiosity among customers.

Conclusion: The Ongoing Art of Creating Unique Flavors

The chapter concludes by emphasizing that the creative process in producing new flavors is an art in continuous evolution. The combination of inspiration, experimentation, and constant adaptation is what makes the experience of creating gelatos that leave an indelible mark on customers' hearts unique.

Strengths and Areas for Improvement: Chapter 6: The Creative Process

Chapter 6: The Creative Process - Evaluation and Development

Strengths:

1. **In-depth Exploration of Sources of Inspiration:**

    - Strength: The in-depth exploration of various sources of inspiration offers a comprehensive guide to stimulate the creativity of gelato makers, providing insights from diverse cultural and personal sources.

2. **Practical Advice on Ingredient Selection:**

    - Strength: Practical advice on ingredient selection provides a clear guide on how to explore and balance ingredients to create unique taste profiles.

3. **Record of Results:**

    - Strength: The emphasis on the importance of keeping a detailed record of results is crucial, providing gelato makers with an essential tool to refine and improve recipes over time.

Areas for Improvement:

1. **In-depth Exploration of Practical Experimentation:**

    - Area for Improvement: A more detailed exploration of how to effectively organize and conduct practical experimentation sessions could further enrich the chapter.

2. **Specific Advice for Launch Events:**

    - Area for Improvement: The inclusion of specific practical advice on how to organize launch events, including associated marketing strategies, could be a useful addition.

3. **Customer Involvement in the Creation of New Flavors:**

    - Area for Improvement: Exploring specific ways to actively involve customers in the new flavor creation phase could make the process more interactive and engaging.

Conclusion: The chapter on the creative process has solid strengths, with detailed insights into sources of inspiration and ingredient selection. However, improvements could be made through more detailed exploration of practical experimentation and specific advice for launch events. Additionally, exploring ways to actively involve customers in the creation of new flavors could make the process more inclusive and interesting for the clientele.

Weaknesses and Errors to Avoid: Chapter 6: The Creative Process

Chapter 6: The Creative Process - Critical Analysis and Errors to Avoid

Weaknesses:

1. **Limited Details on Practical Experimentation:**

- Weakness: The section on practical experimentation might be limited in practical details on how to effectively organize and conduct experimentation sessions.

2. **Absence of Specific Advice for Launch Events:**

   - Weakness: The absence of specific advice for launch events might leave gelato makers less prepared to face the crucial phase of introducing new flavors to the public.

Errors to Avoid:

1. **Lack of Customer Involvement:**

   - Error to Avoid: A potential error is the lack of suggestions on how to actively involve customers in the creative process. Engaging customers can create a stronger bond with the product.

2. **Ignoring the Variety of Local Tastes:**

   - Error to Avoid: Ignoring the variety of local tastes could limit creativity. Incorporating local ingredients and inspirations can make new flavors more appealing to the community.

Conclusion: The chapter on the creative process presents weaknesses in the depth of practical experimentation and the lack of specific advice for launch events. Avoiding the error of not actively involving customers and ignoring the richness of local tastes is crucial to ensure the creation of flavors that resonate with both the clientele and the surrounding culture. Integrating more specific and detailed advice will contribute to addressing these gaps.

Examples and Case Studies: Chapter 6: The Creative Process

Chapter 6: The Creative Process - Illuminated by Examples and Case Studies

Example 1: "Seasonal Creation of Autumnal Gelato" Background: The gelateria "Dolci Delizie" successfully devised a seasonal flavor inspired by autumn. The source of inspiration was the collection of typical autumn fruits, such as apples and walnuts. Creative Process:

- Autumnal Inspiration: Using nature as inspiration, the gelateria experimented with combinations of cooked apples and toasted walnuts to capture the characteristic flavors of autumn.

- Customer Involvement: They involved customers through online surveys, asking them to vote for their favorite combinations of autumnal tastes. Presentation to the Public:

- Themed Launch Event: The gelateria organized an autumnal launch event, decorating the store with seasonal motifs and offering free tastings of the new flavor.

Case Study 2: "Exploring Local Traditions" Background: The gelateria "Gusto Locale" wanted to create a flavor that reflected the culinary traditions of its community. Creative Process:

- Researching Local Traditions: The gelateria conducted research on local culinary traditions, discovering ingredients and flavor combinations typical of the area.

- Collaboration with Local Chefs: They collaborated with local chefs to incorporate traditional techniques and ingredients into the creation of the new flavor. Presentation to the Public:

- Tasting Events with Chefs: For the launch, the gelateria organized tasting events in collaboration with the involved chefs, creating a unique gastronomic experience.

Example 3: "Interactive Flavor of the Month" Background: The gelateria "Gelato Artistico" implemented an interactive approach to flavor creation. Creative Process:

- Monthly Customer Surveys: They instituted monthly online surveys where customers could suggest and vote on the flavor of the month.

- Open Customer Laboratory: Once a month, the gelateria opened its creative laboratory to customers to experiment with ingredients and vote on their favorite combinations. Presentation to the Public:

- Monthly Flavor Announcement: Every month, the gelateria announced the winning flavor, encouraging customers to come and try their creation.

Conclusion: A Vibrant and Engaging Creative Process

These examples and case studies illustrate the unique approach of gelaterias in the creative process. From researching local traditions to an interactive approach with customers, each story demonstrates that creativity is fueled by a connection with the community and innovation.

Future: Chapter 6: The Creative Process

Chapter 6: The Creative Process - Looking to the Future of Taste Innovation

1. **Advanced Technologies in Ingredient Exploration:**

   - Molecular Analysis of Ingredients: Using advanced technologies, gelato makers could explore molecular analysis of ingredients to discover new flavor and texture combinations.

   - Artificial Intelligence for Creative Suggestions: Artificial intelligence could be employed to suggest unexpected ingredient combinations based on customer preferences and culinary trends.

2. **Interdisciplinary Collaborations for Unique Flavors:**

- Collaboration with Chefs, Sommeliers, and Aromatherapists: Interdisciplinary collaborations could become the norm, involving chefs, sommeliers, and aromatherapists to create multisensory taste experiences.
- Open Creative Workshops for the Public: Gelaterias could open creative workshops to the public, allowing customers to actively participate in creating new flavors through expert-guided workshops.

3. **Extreme Customization of Tastes:**

- Personal Taste Profiling: Technological advancements could enable personal taste profiling, allowing customers to create customized gelatos based on their individual preferences.
- 3D Printers for Innovative Decorations: The introduction of 3D printers could be used to create innovative and detailed decorations to enhance the taste experience.

4. **Exploration of Sustainable and Alternative Tastes:**

- Alternative and Sustainable Ingredients: The trend could be the exploration of alternative and sustainable ingredients, such as plant-based milk or natural additives.
- Focus on Ingredient Traceability: Gelaterias could focus on ingredient traceability, transparently communicating the origin and sustainability of each component.

5. **Virtual Taste Creation Experiences:**

- Virtual Taste Creation Labs: Gelaterias could offer virtual taste creation experiences, allowing customers to participate remotely and contribute to the creation of new flavors.
- Virtual Tasting Events with Taste Experts: Virtual tasting events could involve taste experts guiding customers through multisensory experiences in a virtual environment.

Conclusion: Towards an Innovative and Accessible Taste Future

Looking to the future, the creative process in gelato production promises to be a fertile ground for innovation. With the integration of advanced technologies, interdisciplinary collaborations, and a growing focus on sustainability, the future offers exciting opportunities for gelato makers and enthusiasts alike

Chapter 7: Personnel Management - Cultivating a Successful Team in the Gelateria

Introduction: The Importance of Personnel Management The seventh chapter explores the art and science of personnel management in a gelateria. From hiring to ongoing training, we will discover how to cultivate a cohesive and motivated team to ensure the success of your shop.

1. **Effective Hiring Process:**

- Careful Personnel Selection: A practical guide on careful personnel selection, identifying the necessary skills for key roles such as gelato makers, cashiers, and service staff.

- Structured Interviews: How to conduct structured interviews to assess not only technical skills but also attitude and adaptability to the company culture.

2. **Continuous Training and Professional Development:**

- Customized Training Plans: Creating personalized training plans for each team member, identifying areas for improvement and development goals.

- Workshops and Industry Seminars: The importance of encouraging participation in workshops and industry seminars to keep staff updated on the latest trends and techniques.

3. **Effective Communication and Conflict Management:**

- Open Communication Channels: Establishing open communication channels, facilitating the sharing of feedback and ideas between staff and management.

- Constructive Conflict Management: Strategies for addressing conflicts constructively, promoting peaceful resolution and continuous improvement of team dynamics.

4. **Incentives and Recognition:**

- Effective Incentive Programs: How to develop incentive programs that motivate staff, such as monthly recognitions for exceptional performance.

- Celebrating Team Successes: The importance of celebrating team successes, creating a positive and encouraging environment.

5. **Well-being and Work-Life Balance:**

- Wellness Programs: Implementing wellness programs, such as well-structured breaks and team-building activities, to improve satisfaction and productivity.

- Flexibility and Balance: Strategies to offer flexibility in work hours and promote a healthy work-life balance.

Conclusion: A Resilient Team for Sustainable Success The chapter concludes by highlighting that personnel management is a fundamental element for the success of a gelateria. A well-managed, motivated, and well-trained team can create a positive experience for customers and contribute to the sustainable growth of the business.

Strengths and Areas for Improvement: Chapter 7: Personnel Management

Chapter 7: Personnel Management - Analysis and Growth Perspectives

Strengths:

1. Effective Hiring Process:

   - Strength: The guide on careful personnel selection and structured interviews provides a solid foundation to ensure the team is composed of competent individuals aligned with the company culture.

2. **Continuous Training and Professional Development:**

   - Strength: The approach to personalized training plans and encouragement of participation in workshops demonstrates a commitment to cultivating staff skills in the long term.

3. **Effective Communication and Conflict Management:**

   - Strength: Emphasizing open communication and constructive conflict management promotes a healthy and collaborative work environment.

Areas for Improvement:

1. **Incentives and Recognition:**

   - Improvement Area: Further expanding incentive programs could engage staff more deeply, creating a stronger **connection with the company.**

2. **Well**-being and Work-Life Balance:

   - Improvement Area: Further exploring strategies to improve well-being and work-life balance, such as integrating specific team-building activities.

Conclusion: Investing in Human Capital for Sustainable Success The chapter highlights the strength of personnel management but suggests improvement opportunities in incentive programs and team well-being. Investing in human capital through continuous training and a positive work environment is crucial for sustainable success in the gelateria industry.

Weaknesses and Errors to Avoid: Chapter 7: Personnel Management

Chapter 7: Personnel Management - Identification of Weak Points and Errors to Avoid

Weaknesses:

1. **Effective Hiring Process:**

   - Weakness: The guide on careful personnel selection could benefit from practical examples or scenarios to better illustrate the application of principles.

2. **Incentives and Recognition:**

   - Weakness: The section on incentive programs could be generic. Adding specific examples or case studies would enhance understanding of best practices.

Errors to Avoid:

1. **Effective Communication and Conflict Management:**

   - Error to Avoid: Not specifically addressing the challenges of virtual communication and conflict management in a remote work environment could reduce the effectiveness of proposed strategies.

2. **Well-being and Work-Life Balance:**

   - Error to Avoid: Not providing practical examples or specific suggestions for improving well-being and work-life balance could limit the applicability of proposed strategies.

Conclusion: A Refined Approach for Effective Management The chapter points out weaknesses in the personnel selection guide and the section on incentive programs. Adding practical examples and addressing specific challenges of personnel management in a virtual context would positively impact the effectiveness of proposed strategies. A more refined approach would contribute to creating a more resilient and dynamic work environment.

Examples and Case Studies: Chapter 7: Personnel Management

Chapter 7: Personnel Management - Illuminated by Examples and Case Studies

Example 1: "Building a Winning Team" Background: The gelateria "Art of Gelato" has implemented a personnel selection process that contributed to the formation of a highly competent and motivated team.

Key Strategies:

- Careful Selection: Using structured interviews and practical tests, the gelateria selected candidates with not only technical skills but also a positive attitude and genuine interest in the industry.

- Personalized Training: After hiring, a personalized training plan was developed for each team member, allowing them to grow both professionally and personally.

- Open Communication: The gelateria established open communication channels, creating a culture where staff feel comfortable sharing ideas and feedback.

Results: The team's cohesion and dedication have translated into improved customer satisfaction and increased sales. The positive work environment has also contributed to low staff turnover.

Example 2: "Incentive Magic at Gelato Haven" Background: "Gelato Haven" introduced a creative incentive program to boost staff motivation and engagement.

Key Strategies:

- Monthly Recognition: The gelateria implemented a monthly recognition program where the team votes for the most outstanding performer, creating a sense of camaraderie and acknowledgment.

- Surprise Incentives: In addition to regular recognition, surprise incentives, such as extra time off or small bonuses, are awarded for exceptional efforts or innovative ideas.

Results: The incentive program has significantly increased staff motivation, leading to improved customer service and a positive atmosphere within the team. The surprise incentives keep the team excited and committed to delivering their best.

Case Study: "Balancing Act - A Focus on Well-being at Frosty Delights" Background: "Frosty Delights" prioritized staff well-being and work-life balance, leading to positive outcomes for both employees and the business.

Key Strategies:

- Structured Breaks: The gelateria implemented well-structured breaks to allow staff to recharge and maintain peak performance during working hours.

- Team-Building Activities: Regular team-building activities, such as monthly outings or collaborative projects, fostered a sense of community among the staff.

Results: The focus on well-being has resulted in a more content and energized team, leading to improved productivity and creativity. The positive work atmosphere has also contributed to increased customer satisfaction.

Conclusion: Real-World Success Stories The examples and case studies illustrate the practical application of personnel management strategies in gelaterias. By learning from the experiences of successful establishments, one can adapt and implement similar approaches to create a thriving and harmonious work environment.

Opinions on the Chapter 7 Content: Personnel Management

Chapter 7: Personnel Management - Nuccio's Insights and Opinions

Effective Hiring Process:

- **Nuccio's Opinion:** The emphasis on careful personnel selection aligns with Nuccio's belief in the importance of having a team that shares the same values and commitment to the company's mission.

- **Suggestion:** Nuccio suggests including anecdotes or real-life examples to make the hiring process guidance more relatable and applicable to different situations.

Continuous Training and Professional Development:

- **Nuccio's Opinion:** Nuccio appreciates the focus on personalized training plans, emphasizing the unique needs of each team member.

- **Suggestion:** Nuccio recommends expanding on the role of mentors or senior team members in facilitating the professional development of newer staff.

Effective Communication and Conflict Management:

- **Nuccio's Opinion:** Nuccio agrees with the emphasis on open communication and constructive conflict management for a positive work environment.

- **Suggestion:** Nuccio suggests addressing the challenges of communication and conflict management in a virtual or remote work context, considering the evolving nature of work arrangements.

Incentives and Recognition:

- **Nuccio's Opinion:** Nuccio sees the value in recognizing and incentivizing staff for their efforts.

- **Suggestion:** Nuccio suggests exploring specific examples or case studies to inspire creative incentive programs tailored to the gelateria industry.

Well-being and Work-Life Balance:

- **Nuccio's Opinion:** Nuccio appreciates the importance placed on well-being and work-life balance.

- **Suggestion:** Nuccio recommends delving deeper into practical strategies for implementing wellness programs, considering the unique challenges of the gelateria work environment.

Conclusion: A Valuable Guide with Room for Enrichment Nuccio finds the content valuable, aligning with his philosophy of fostering a positive and inclusive work environment. He provides insightful suggestions to enhance the chapter, making it even more applicable to the diverse scenarios gelateria owners may encounter.

I hope these insights and analyses align with your expectations, Nuccio. Feel free to share any additional thoughts or preferences for further refinement!

Chapter 8: The Magic of Seasons –

Creating Unique Taste Experiences for Every Time of the Year

Introduction: Celebrating the Diversity of Seasons

The eighth chapter explores how the gelateria can embrace the magic of seasons to offer unique taste experiences. From the freshness of spring to the warm embrace of winter, we will discover how to tailor your offerings to the distinctive characteristics of each season.

1. **Spring: Renewal of Tastes and Colors**

   - Floral and Fruity Flavors: Introduction of light and fresh flavors inspired by spring, such as elderflower, strawberries, and peach.

   - Vibrant Color Palette: Use of vibrant colors in presenting the gelato to capture the rejuvenating atmosphere of spring.

2. **Summer: Exploring Refreshing Flavors**

   - Fruit Gelatos: Incorporation of fruit gelatos like melon, watermelon, and lemon to provide refreshing options during hot days.

   - Sorbets and Granitas: Introduction of sorbets and granitas with intense and thirst-quenching flavors.

3. **Autumn: Depth of Warm and Spicy Flavors**

   - Pumpkin and Cinnamon Gelatos: Creation of comforting flavors like pumpkin, cinnamon, and baked apple.

   - Autumnal Decorations: Use of autumnal decorations like chocolate leaves and nuts to enrich the presentation.

4. Winter: Comfort and Sweetness

   - Hot Chocolate Gelatos: Offering hot chocolate gelatos and winter desserts to satisfy comfort cravings.

   - Festive Limited Editions: Creation of limited-edition festive gelatos inspired by holiday and winter traditions.

5. Seasonal Events and Collaborations

   - Gelateria Seasonal Festivals: Organizing seasonal festivals to celebrate new creations and engage the community.

- Collaborations with Local Producers: Collaborating with local producers to obtain fresh and seasonal ingredients.

Conclusion: Transforming Seasons into Unforgettable Experiences

The chapter concludes that the magic of seasons can be captured through creativity in flavor selection, captivating presentation, and active community involvement. Transforming seasons into unforgettable taste experiences adds a touch of charm and variety to your gelateria.

Strengths and Areas for Improvement: Chapter 8: The Magic of Seasons

Chapter 8: The Magic of Seasons - Analysis of Strengths and Challenges

Strengths:

1. **Spring: Renewal of Tastes and Colors:**

   - Strength: Introducing fresh tastes and vibrant colors captures the essence of spring, offering a unique taste experience.

2. **Summer: Exploring Refreshing Flavors:**

   - Strength: Incorporating fruit gelatos and sorbets to address summer heat demonstrates a practical response to customer needs during the warm season.

3. **Autumn: Depth of Warm and Spicy Flavors:**

   - Strength: Creating comforting flavors and autumnal decorations highlights the ability to adapt to seasonal preferences and offer a nature-connected experience.

4. **Winter: Comfort and Sweetness:**

   - Strength: Offering hot chocolate gelatos and festive limited editions showcases versatility in creating a cozy and festive atmosphere.

5. **Seasonal Events and Collaborations:**

   - Strength: Organizing seasonal festivals and collaborating with local producers contributes to community connection and broadens offerings.

Areas for Improvement:

1. **Spring: Renewal of Tastes and Colors:**

   - Improvement Area: Further exploring the use of specific local spring ingredients for a deeper connection with the region.

2. **Summer: Exploring Refreshing Flavors:**

   - Improvement Area: Introducing sugar-free or low-calorie options could attract a broader customer base during summer.

3. **Autumn: Depth of Warm and Spicy Flavors:**

   - Improvement Area: Considering the inclusion of bolder variants, such as gelatos with exotic spice flavors, for a distinctive touch.

4. **Winter: Comfort and Sweetness:**

   - Improvement Area: Exploring vegan or lactose-free options to cater to a wider range of dietary preferences during winter festivities.

5. **Seasonal Events and Collaborations:**

   - Improvement Area: Expanding the scope of seasonal festivals could further engage the community and generate interest.

Conclusion: Refining the Art of Seasonal Gelateria

The chapter reveals notable strengths in addressing different seasons, but there are opportunities for improvement through exploring bolder variants and adapting to specific dietary needs. Continuing to refine the art of seasonal gelateria will ensure an exceptional taste experience for all customers.

Weaknesses and Errors to Avoid: Chapter 8: The Magic of Seasons

Chapter 8: The Magic of Seasons - Identifying Weaknesses and Errors to Avoid

Weaknesses:

1. **Spring: Renewal of Tastes and Colors:**

   - Weakness: Lack of in-depth exploration of the specific use of local ingredients may limit the authenticity of the spring offering.

2. **Summer: Exploring Refreshing Flavors:**

   - Weakness: Absence of low-calorie or sugar-free options may not fully meet the demand for lighter alternatives during summer.

3. **Autumn: Depth of Warm and Spicy Flavors:**

   - Weakness: Lack of bolder variants may reduce the ability to stand out and offer unique experiences.

4. **Winter: Comfort and Sweetness:**

   - Weakness: Not offering vegan or lactose-free options may limit attractiveness during winter festivities.

5. **Seasonal Events and Collaborations:**

- Weakness: The need to expand the reach of seasonal festivals to further engage the community and attract participants.

Errors to Avoid:

1. **Spring: Renewal of Tastes and Colors:**

   - Error to Avoid: Neglecting the opportunity to create connections with local producers may diminish the authenticity of the spring proposal.

2. **Summer: Exploring Refreshing Flavors:**

   - Error to Avoid: Not addressing the needs of customers with specific dietary preferences may limit the target market during summer.

3. **Autumn: Depth of Warm and Spicy Flavors:**

   - Error to Avoid: Not experimenting with bolder flavors may reduce the ability to attract customers seeking unique experiences.

4. **Winter: Comfort and Sweetness:**

   - Error to Avoid: Not offering vegan or lactose-free options may exclude a significant portion of the winter market.

5. **Seasonal Events and Collaborations:**

   - Error to Avoid: Not extending the scope of seasonal festivals may limit the opportunity to actively engage the community and create a festive atmosphere.

Conclusion: Strengthening and Enriching Seasonal Offerings

Identifying weaknesses and errors to avoid highlights the need to strengthen the authenticity of seasonal proposals and respond more targetedly to specific audience needs. Continuing to avoid these errors and improving will lead to a stronger and more attractive seasonal offering for customers.

Examples and Case Studies: Chapter 8: The Magic of Seasons

Chapter 8: The Magic of Seasons - Illuminated by Examples and Case Studies

Example 1: "

Blooming Spring" Background: The gelateria "Sweet Spring" captured the essence of spring through collaboration with local farmers. Key Strategies:

- Local Ingredients: Using local flowers and herbs to create unique gelatos that reflect the freshness of the season.

- Inn Events: Organizing events at local inns to allow customers to meet farmers and understand the cultivation process of ingredients.

Case Study 2: "

Fruity Summer" Background: The gelateria "Fresh Summer" expanded its summer offering with a series of fruit-based flavors. Key Strategies:

- Artisanal Fruit Gelatos: Creating artisanal fruit gelatos with fresh seasonal fruit from local suppliers.
- Summer Festival: Organizing a summer festival with free tastings to promote new flavors and engage the community.

Example 3: "

Cozy Autumn" Background: The gelateria "Sweet Autumn" transformed the changing leaves into a taste experience. Key Strategies:

- Spiced Gelatos: Introducing spiced gelatos such as cinnamon, ginger, and nutmeg to capture the autumnal atmosphere.
- Thematic Decorations: Using autumnal decorations, such as chocolate leaves and pumpkin candies, to enrich the presentation.

Case Study 4:

"Warm Winter" Background: The gelateria "Warm Winter" made winter cozier with a selection of hot chocolate gelatos. Key Strategies:

- Hot Chocolate Gelatos: Offering hot chocolate gelatos with variations like dark chocolate and milk chocolate.
- Festive Limited Editions: Creating festive limited editions, such as cinnamon and gingerbread gelatos, during winter holidays.

Conclusion: Creating Unique Taste Moments for Every Season

Examples and case studies demonstrate how the magic of seasons can be captured through local collaborations, new flavor introductions, and themed events. Creating unique taste moments for each season not only enriches the gelateria's offering but also builds deeper connections with the local community.

Future and Perspectives: Chapter 8: The Magic of Seasons

Chapter 8: The Magic of Seasons - Exploring the Future and Innovative Perspectives

1. **Emerging Technologies for Customer Experience:**

   - Interactive Digital Menus: Implementation of interactive digital menus allowing customers to customize their gelatos based on seasonal preferences.

- Augmented Reality for Presentation: Use of augmented reality to innovatively present new seasonal flavors, enabling customers to "virtually taste" before ordering.

2. **Sustainability and Seasonal Ingredients:**

   - Certified Local Suppliers: Increased collaboration with certified local suppliers to ensure the freshness and sustainable sourcing of seasonal ingredients.
   - Zero-Impact Gelatos: Introduction of zero-impact gelatos packaged in eco-friendly materials, reducing resource consumption.

3. **Experiential and Social Events:**

   - Gelato Creation Workshops: Organization of interactive workshops where customers can create their own personalized gelatos using seasonal ingredients.
   - Seasonal Theme Nights: Hosting seasonal theme nights with live music, tastings, and presentations of new flavors.

4. **Advanced Customization:**

   - Customer Taste Profiling: Use of advanced technologies to create individual customer taste profiles, enabling personalized recommendations based on seasonal preferences.
   - Extreme Customization Options: Introduction of extreme customization options, such as the ability to add unexpected ingredients for unique experiences.

5. **Community Engagement and Social Responsibility:**

   - Local Engagement Programs: Expansion of local engagement programs, involving the community in ingredient cultivation or joint event organization.
   - Seasonal Charity Projects: Implementation of seasonal charity projects, connecting new flavors to local support initiatives.

Conclusion: Embracing Innovation and Connection with the Community

Exploring the future of the magic of seasons requires a commitment to innovation, sustainability, and active community engagement. Embracing these perspectives will ensure that your gelateria continues to offer unique and meaningful taste experiences for all seasons, creating stronger connections with customers and the community.

Chapter 9: Palate Education - Refining Taste Skills for an Amazing Gelato Experience

Introduction: The Importance of Palate Education The ninth chapter explores the crucial role of palate education in the creation and appreciation of high-quality gelato. We will discover how refining taste skills not only enhances your experience but also guides customers towards more conscious choices.

1. **Guided Tasting of Basic Flavors:**

   - Basic Taste Profile: A detailed analysis of basic tastes such as sweet, salty, bitter, sour, and umami to understand the complexity of the palate.

   - Direct Comparisons: Comparative tasting exercises to distinguish nuances between different varieties of sweetness or varying levels of bitterness.

2. **Exploration of Aromas and Scents:**

   - Aromatic Associations: Learning associations between aromas and tastes, facilitating the creation of gelato with distinctive aromatic profiles.

   - Odor Recognition: Exercises to recognize and identify a wide range of scents, enhancing the ability to grasp aromatic nuances in gelato.

3. **Tasting Various Textures:**

   - Gelato Structure: Exploration of the consistency and structure of gelato, understanding how factors like creaminess and lightness influence the taste experience.

   - Texture Pairings: Creating gelato with creative texture pairings, such as combining crunchiness and creaminess.

4. **Identification of Ingredient Origins:**

   - Journey through Origins: Exploration of the origins of key ingredients, developing a deeper understanding of regional and seasonal influences.

   - Geographical Pairings: Associating tastes and ingredients with specific regions to create gelato that tells a story through the palate.

5. **Advanced Gelato Courses:**

   - Specialized Tastings: Participation in specialized gelato tastings, deepening knowledge of specific varieties and production techniques.

   - Creating Complex Gelato: Experimentation with advanced ingredients and techniques to create complex and sophisticated gelato.

Conclusion: Guiding the Palate towards an Elevated Gelato Experience The chapter concludes that palate education is essential for anyone wishing to create high-quality gelato and guide customers towards a deeper appreciation of the world of tastes. Refining taste skills contributes not only to improving your ability to create extraordinary gelato but also to elevating the entire gelato experience for you and your customers.

Strengths and Perspectives: Chapter 9 - Palate Education

Chapter 9: Palate Education - Highlighting Strengths and Looking to the Future of Taste Skills

Strengths:

1. **Guided Tasting of Basic Flavors:**

   - Strength: In-depth analysis of basic tastes provides a solid foundation for understanding taste nuances in gelato.

2. **Exploration of Aromas and Scents:**

   - Strength: The association between aromas and tastes enhances creativity in creating distinctive and memorable aromatic profiles.

3. **Tasting Various Textures:**

   - Strength: Understanding gelato structure and experimenting with texture pairings enriches the sensory experience.

4. **Identification of Ingredient Origins:**

   - Strength: In-depth knowledge of ingredient origins fosters a deeper connection with regional and seasonal influences.

5. **Advanced Gelato Courses:**

   - Strength: Participation in advanced gelato courses offers the opportunity to explore techniques and deepen knowledge, improving the ability to create complex gelato.

Future Perspectives:

1. **Innovative Technologies for Tasting:**

   - Future Perspective: Exploring innovative technologies, such as virtual reality, could open new dimensions in guided tasting, offering a more immersive experience.

2. **Digital Palate Education:**

   - Future Perspective: Creating digital educational resources could enable a broader dissemination of palate education, reaching a wider audience.

3. **Deepening Sensorial Associations:**

- Future Perspective: Deepening sensorial associations could lead to greater experimentation with bold and surprising flavor combinations.

4. **Exploring Global Taste Trends:**

   - Future Perspective: Monitoring and adapting to global taste trends could ensure constant innovation and attention to emerging preferences.

5. **Collaborations with Taste Experts:**

   - Future Perspective: Collaborating with taste experts in related fields, such as molecular gastronomy, could lead to innovative discoveries and approaches in gelato creation.

Conclusion: Continuous Education and Adapting to Trends The chapter emphasizes that valuing the strengths of palate education is essential for enhancing taste skills. Looking to the future involves adapting to new technologies and global trends, ensuring continuous and stimulating education that constantly enriches your experience in the world of gelato.

Weaknesses and Mistakes to Avoid: Chapter 9 - Palate Education

Chapter 9: Palate Education - Overcoming Weaknesses and Avoiding Common Mistakes

Weaknesses:

1. **Guided Tasting of Basic Flavors:**

   - Weakness: Lack of depth in analysis may limit understanding of nuances in basic tastes, affecting the creation of complex taste profiles.

2. **Exploration of Aromas and Scents:**

   - Weakness: Insufficient attention to the association between aromas and tastes may reduce creativity in creating unique aromatic experiences.

3. **Tasting Various Textures:**

   - Weakness: Limited experimentation with texture pairings may restrict the ability to offer diverse sensory experiences.

4. **Identification of Ingredient Origins:**

   - Weakness: Thorough knowledge of ingredient origins is crucial; lacking such knowledge could compromise the connection with regional influences.

5. **Advanced Gelato Courses:**

   - Weakness: Lack of access to advanced courses may limit the opportunity to explore techniques and deepen knowledge.

Mistakes to Avoid:

1. **Unintegrated Innovative Technologies:**

   - Mistake to Avoid: Adopting innovative technologies without considering their effective integration into daily practice may lead to a lack of adoption.

2. **Underestimating the Importance of Digital Education:**

   - Mistake to Avoid: Underestimating the potential of digital educational resources may limit the spread of palate education to a broader audience.

3. **Lack of Depth in Sensorial Associations:**

   - Mistake to Avoid: Insufficient depth in sensorial associations may limit creativity in creating new gelato flavors.

4. **Ignoring Global Taste Trends:**

   - Mistake to Avoid: Ignoring global taste trends may lead to a lack of innovation and attention to emerging preferences.

5. **Failure to Collaborate with Taste Experts:**

   - Mistake to Avoid: Failure to collaborate with taste experts may restrict access to new knowledge and innovative approaches.

Conclusion: Overcoming Challenges for Excellence in Palate Education The chapter concludes that overcoming weaknesses and avoiding common mistakes is crucial to ensuring excellence in palate education. Attention to details such as experimentation, integration of technologies, and collaboration with taste experts will contribute to the continuous improvement of taste skills.

Errors and Weaknesses to Avoid: Chapter 9 - Palate Education

Chapter 9: Palate Education - Avoiding Common Errors and Overcoming Weaknesses

Common Errors:

1. **Inadequate Analysis of Basic Flavors:**

   - Error: Failing to conduct a thorough analysis of basic flavors may result in a limited understanding of taste nuances, hindering the creation of sophisticated gelato profiles.

2. **Neglecting Aroma-Taste Associations:**

   - Error: Overlooking the association between aromas and tastes can limit creativity in crafting distinctive aromatic experiences.

3. **Restricting Texture Pairings:**

   - Error: Avoiding experimentation with texture pairings may lead to a lack of diversity in sensory experiences.

4. **Insufficient Knowledge of Ingredient Origins:**
   - Error: Failing to delve into the origins of ingredients can weaken the connection with regional and seasonal influences, impacting the storytelling aspect of gelato creation.

5. **Limited Access to Advanced Courses:**
   - Error: Being unable to access advanced gelato courses may restrict opportunities for skill development and knowledge enrichment.

Overcoming Weaknesses:

1. **Comprehensive Basic Flavors Analysis:**
   - Solution: Conducting comprehensive analyses of basic flavors through guided tastings and comparisons will deepen understanding and enhance taste skills.

2. **Emphasizing Aroma-Taste Relationships:**
   - Solution: Prioritizing the exploration of aroma-taste associations will foster creativity and contribute to the development of unique aromatic profiles.

3. **Expanding Texture Experimentation:**
   - Solution: Actively seeking opportunities to experiment with various texture pairings will broaden the range of sensory experiences offered through gelato.

4. **In-Depth Ingredient Origin Exploration:**
   - Solution: Taking the time to thoroughly explore the origins of ingredients ensures a strong connection with regional influences, enriching the storytelling aspect of gelato creation.

5. **Seeking Alternative Learning Opportunities:**
   - Solution: Exploring alternative avenues for learning, such as online courses or collaborations with experts, can provide access to advanced knowledge and techniques.

Conclusion: Continuous Improvement for Palate Mastery The chapter concludes by highlighting the importance of avoiding common errors and overcoming weaknesses in palate education. Embracing solutions and seeking continuous improvement will contribute to mastery in the art of gelato creation

Chapter 10: Social Media and Community

Chapter 10: Social Media and Community - Building a Strong and Connecting Digital Presence

1. **Social Platforms and Gelaterias:**

   - Key Role: Explore the potential of platforms like Instagram, Facebook, and TikTok to share captivating images of gelatos, engage the community, and promote special events.

2. **Creating Engaging Content:**

   - Effective Strategies: Develop engaging visual content, including photos and videos showcasing the gelato-making process, new creations, and behind-the-scenes moments to emotionally connect with the audience.

3. **Engaging the Community:**

   - Active Participation: Create engaging polls, questions, and challenges to encourage interaction within the community, fostering a sense of participation and belonging.

4. **Collaborations with Influencers:**

   - Strategic Benefits: Collaborate with influencers in the food and lifestyle industry to increase visibility, reach new audiences, and receive authentic reviews.

5. **Live Social Media Events:**

   - Real-time Interaction: Organize live events to share new creations, answer community questions, and engage the audience in real-time.

6. **Use of Customized Hashtags:**

   - Identity Building: Create and promote customized hashtags to solidify the brand's identity and encourage the community to share their gelato-related experiences.

7. **Interactive Stories:**

   - Direct Engagement: Utilize interactive stories on platforms like Instagram for polls, quizzes, and dynamic content that encourages active community participation.

8. **Responding to Feedback:**

   - Transparency and Listening: Monitor customer feedback on social media and respond transparently, demonstrating a genuine commitment to continuous improvement.

9. **Educational Content on the Art of Gelato:**

- Sharing Knowledge: Create educational content that shares the history of gelato, production techniques, and behind-the-scenes insights to spark interest and appreciation.

10. Creating an Online Community:

- Relationship Building: Foster an online community where gelato enthusiasts can share experiences, tips, and recipes, creating a virtual hub of connection. Conclusion: Harnessing the Power of Digital Connections Building a strong digital presence through social media and the creation of an online community is essential to connect with the audience, promote interaction, and amplify the brand's impact. Harnessing the power of digital connections will contribute to maintaining a meaningful relationship with the gelato-loving community.

Strengths and Perspectives: Chapter 10: Social Media and Community

Chapter 10: Social Media and Community - Emphasizing Strengths and Looking to the Future Current Strengths:

1. Compelling Visual Communication:

- Strength: The effective use of captivating photos and videos on social media captures users' attention, creating a visually impactful and stimulating experience.

2. Active Community Engagement:

- Strength: Creating polls, challenges, and interactive content stimulates interaction, fostering a sense of active participation within the community.

3. Successful Collaborations with Influencers:

- Strength: Collaborations with influencers in the food and lifestyle industry amplify the brand's visibility, reaching new audiences and solidifying its reputation.

4. Attentive Response to Feedback:

- Strength: Promptly responding to customer feedback demonstrates transparency and a genuine commitment to continuous improvement.

5. Engaging Educational Content:

- Strength: Sharing educational content on the art of gelato contributes to generating interest, deepening the emotional connection with the community. Future Perspectives:

6. Exploring New Emerging Platforms:

- Future Perspective: Exploring new emerging platforms could offer opportunities to reach new audience segments, expanding digital presence.

7. **Integration of Interactive Technologies:**

   - Future Perspective: Integrating interactive technologies, such as augmented reality, could further elevate the digital experience, engaging the community in innovative ways.

8. **Deepening Personalization of Experiences:**

   - Future Perspective: Deepening the personalization of digital experiences, through exclusive offerings or customized filters, could create deeper bonds with the community.

9. **Development of Multilingual Content:**

   - Future Perspective: Creating multilingual content could expand the global audience, allowing more effective communication with diverse communities.

10. **Further Exploration of Real-time Stories:**

    - Future Perspective: Exploring additional possibilities in real-time stories on platforms like Instagram could keep the audience engaged and connected. Conclusion: Guiding Digital Evolution with Flexibility and Innovation Emphasizing current strengths and looking to the future with innovative perspectives will guide digital evolution in a flexible and adaptable manner. Utilizing emerging opportunities will ensure a continually cutting-edge digital presence in line with community expectations.

Weaknesses and Mistakes to Avoid: Chapter 10: Social Media and Community

Chapter 10: Social Media and Community - Overcoming Weaknesses and Avoiding Common Mistakes Weaknesses:

1. **Inconsistency in Online Branding:**

   - Weakness: Using images, tones, or communication styles online that do not reflect the identity and branding of your gelateria.

2. **Ignoring or Underestimating Community Engagement:**

   - Weakness: Not responding to comments, reviews, or messages on the social media page.

3. **Excessive Promotion and Lack of Authenticity:**

   - Weakness: Posting only promotional content without sharing behind-the-scenes, personal stories, or authentic moments.

4. **Ignoring Social Media Analytics:**

- Weakness: Not monitoring social media analytics to assess the effectiveness of your strategies.

5. **Lack of Variation in Content:**

   - Weakness: Repeating the same types of content without variation.

6. **Not Leveraging Online Collaborations:**

   - Weakness: Not collaborating with other brands or online influencers to expand visibility.

7. **Inadequate Response to Criticism:**

   - Weakness: Responding negatively or defensively to negative reviews.

8. **Ignoring New Emerging Platforms:**

   - Weakness: Limiting yourself to the most popular social platforms without exploring new emerging channels. Mistakes to Avoid:

9. **Solution:** Maintain consistency in your online approach, reflecting the same values and atmosphere that customers experience when visiting the gelateria.

10. **Solution:** Keep active engagement with your online community, respond to questions, appreciate feedback, and participate in conversations to create a positive relationship with customers.

11. **Solution:** Balance promotion with authentic content showcasing behind-the-scenes, the gelato production process, and daily life in the gelateria.

12. **Solution:** Use available analytics tools to understand which types of content work best, the optimal times for posting, and how to improve interaction.

13. **Solution:** Experiment with different content formats such as photos, videos, stories, and polls to maintain your audience's interest.

14. **Solution:** Explore collaborations with other local businesses or influencers in your area to increase reach and attract new audiences.

15. **Solution:** Address criticism professionally, offering solutions or constructive responses and demonstrating a commitment to improvement.

16. **Solution:** Stay updated on new trends and platforms, evaluating whether they align with your gelateria's goals and audience.

Conclusion: Overcoming Challenges for a Stronger Digital Presence The chapter concludes that overcoming weaknesses and avoiding common mistakes is crucial for building a stronger digital presence. Attention to details such as consistent branding, active community engagement, and varied content will contribute to the success of the gelateria's online strategy.

Chapter 10: Social Media and Community - Avoiding Common Errors and Overcoming
Weaknesses Common Errors:

1. **Inadequate Analysis of Basic Flavors:**

   - Error: Failing to conduct a thorough analysis of basic flavors may result in a limited understanding of taste nuances, hindering the creation of sophisticated gelato profiles.

2. **Neglecting Aroma-Taste Associations:**

   - Error: Overlooking the association between aromas and tastes can limit creativity in crafting distinctive aromatic experiences.

3. **Restricting Texture Pairings:**

   - Error: Avoiding experimentation with texture pairings may lead to a lack of diversity in sensory experiences.

4. **Insufficient Knowledge of Ingredient Origins:**

   - Error: Failing to delve into the origins of ingredients can weaken the connection with regional and seasonal influences, impacting the storytelling aspect of gelato creation.

5. **Limited Access to Advanced Courses:**

   - Error: Being unable to access advanced gelato courses may restrict opportunities for skill development and knowledge enrichment.

Overcoming Weaknesses:

1. **Comprehensive Basic Flavors Analysis:**

   - Solution: Conducting comprehensive analyses of basic flavors through guided tastings and comparisons will deepen understanding and enhance taste skills.

2. **Emphasizing Aroma-Taste Relationships:**

   - Solution: Prioritizing the exploration of aroma-taste associations will foster creativity and contribute to the development of unique aromatic profiles.

3. **Expanding Texture Experimentation:**

   - Solution: Actively seeking opportunities to experiment with various texture pairings will broaden the range of sensory experiences offered through gelato.

4. **In-Depth Ingredient Origin Exploration:**

- Solution: Taking the time to thoroughly explore the origins of ingredients ensures a strong connection with regional influences, enriching the storytelling aspect of gelato creation.

5. **Seeking Alternative Learning Opportunities**:

   - Solution: Exploring alternative avenues for learning, such as online courses or collaborations with experts, can provide access to advanced knowledge and techniques.

Conclusion: Continuous Improvement for Palate Mastery The chapter concludes by highlighting the importance of avoiding common errors and overcoming weaknesses in palate education. Embracing solutions and seeking continuous improvement will contribute to mastery in the art of gelato creation

Chapter 11: Sustainability in the Gelateria of the Future

In this chapter, we will delve deeply into how to integrate sustainable practices into the management of a gelateria. Sustainability is not just an ethical imperative but can also be a distinctive element that attracts conscious consumers. Let's structure the chapter:

1. **Responsible Ingredient Selection:**

   - Sustainable Origins: Explore the sourcing of ingredients, prioritizing suppliers following sustainable and fair trade agricultural practices.

   - Seasonal Ingredients: Use seasonal ingredients to reduce the ecological footprint and promote freshness.

2. **Eco-Friendly Packaging:**

   - Sustainable Materials: Examine biodegradable or recyclable packaging options to reduce environmental impact.

   - Recycling: Implement recycling programs for packaging and engage customers in adopting sustainable practices.

3. **Energy and Waste Reduction:**

   - Energy Efficiency: Adopt low-energy consumption technologies and equipment in ice cream production.

- Waste Reduction: Implement strategies to minimize ingredient waste during production and reduce unsold food.

4. **Innovations in Production:**

   - Recycling Systems: Explore recycling and reuse systems for by-products of ice cream production.

   - Low Environmental Impact Processes: Invest in technologies that reduce water and energy use in production.

5. **Community Engagement:**

   - Environmental Education: Conduct educational programs for the community on sustainability, involving customers in the gelateria's eco-friendly mission.

   - Charity Initiatives: Collaborate with local environmental organizations and contribute to charity initiatives for the environment.

6. **Social and Ethical Sustainability:**

   - Working Conditions: Ensure fair working conditions for gelateria staff.

   - Community Involvement: Actively participate in social initiatives supporting the local community.

7. **Certifications and Transparency:**

   - Environmental Certifications: Obtain recognized environmental certifications to demonstrate commitment to sustainability.

   - Transparency: Be transparent about adopted sustainable practices, communicating clearly with customers.

8. **Research and Innovation:**

   - Experimentation with Alternative Ingredients: Explore alternative ingredients, such as plant-based milks and sugar substitutes, to reduce environmental impact and offer options for specific dietary needs.

9. **Eco-Marketing:**

   - Sustainable Communication: Create marketing strategies focused on sustainability to inform customers about the gelateria's eco-friendly choices.

   - Customer Incentives: Offer discounts or promotions for customers adopting sustainable practices, such as using reusable cups.

10. **Monitoring and Evaluation:**

- Impact Analysis: Implement monitoring systems to assess the impact of adopted sustainable practices and make continuous improvements.

This chapter aims to guide the reader through a detailed and practical view of sustainable strategies, demonstrating that sustainability not only benefits the environment but can also be a competitive advantage for the gelateria of the future.

Strengths and Areas for Improvement: Chapter 11: Sustainability

Strengths:

1. **Responsible Ingredient Sourcing:**

   - **Strength:** The gelateria has established relationships with local suppliers following sustainable and fair trade practices.

   - **Area for Improvement:** Expand the range of suppliers to include small local producers and further promote sustainable agriculture.

2. **Energy Efficiency and Waste Reduction:**

   - **Strength:** The gelateria has adopted low-energy consumption equipment and implemented strategies to reduce ingredient waste.

   - **Area for Improvement:** Continuously monitor and optimize processes to maximize efficiency and further reduce waste.

3. **Active Community Engagement:**

   - **Strength:** The gelateria regularly organizes educational events on sustainability, actively engaging the community.

   - **Area for Improvement:** Expand engagement initiatives by involving local schools or organizing collaborative workshops with other sustainable businesses.

4. **Transparent Communication:**

   - **Strength:** The gelateria is transparent about its sustainable practices, clearly communicating with customers.

   - **Area for Improvement:** Create visually engaging educational materials to highlight sustainable practices during customer visits.

Areas for Improvement:

1. **Environmental Certifications and Transparency:**

   - **Area for Improvement:** Obtain and further promote recognized environmental certifications to enhance the credibility of the gelateria's sustainable practices.

2. **Employee Education:**

- **Area for Improvement:** Implement periodic training programs for staff on sustainability, actively involving them in eco-friendly initiatives.

3. **Research and Innovation:**

   - **Area for Improvement:** Invest in continuous research to identify new alternative ingredients and innovative processes to further enhance sustainability.

4. **Effective Eco-Marketing:**

   - **Area for Improvement:** Review and optimize sustainable marketing strategies to ensure alignment with the gelateria's commitment to sustainability.

5. **Environmental Impact Monitoring:**

   - **Area for Improvement:** Implement more advanced environmental impact monitoring systems to assess the detailed impact of sustainable practices.

Addressing these areas for improvement can further strengthen the gelateria's commitment to sustainability, improving the consistency and effectiveness of eco-friendly practices.

Weaknesses: Chapter 11: Sustainability

Weaknesses:

1. **Responsible Ingredient Sourcing:**

   - **Weakness:** The gelateria may depend on a limited number of suppliers, increasing the risk of supply chain instability.

   - **Possible Improvement:** Diversify the supplier base to reduce the risk of supply disruptions and further promote diversity and inclusivity.

2. **Energy Efficiency and Waste Reduction:**

   - **Weakness:** Energy efficiency could be further optimized, and waste could be reduced more aggressively.

   - **Possible Improvement:** Conduct a detailed analysis of production processes to identify additional areas for improvement in terms of efficiency and waste reduction.

3. **Active Community Engagement:**

   - **Weakness:** There might be a lack of engagement with specific demographic groups in the community.

   - **Possible Improvement:** Identify specific interest groups in the community and create targeted engagement initiatives to actively include them.

4. **Transparent Communication:**

- **Weakness:** Transparency could be improved in communicating challenges faced in the pursuit of sustainability.
- **Possible Improvement:** Openly share challenges faced, demonstrating commitment and transparency to build trust with customers.

5. **Environmental Certifications and Transparency:**
   - **Weakness:** The gelateria may not have yet obtained recognized environmental certifications.
   - **Possible Improvement:** Research and adhere to respected environmental certifications to confirm and strengthen the commitment to sustainability.

6. **Employee Education:**
   - **Weakness:** There may be a lack of awareness among staff regarding the importance of sustainability.
   - **Possible Improvement:** Implement regular training programs for staff, highlighting the importance of sustainability and actively involving them in initiatives.

7. Research and Innovation:
   - **Weakness:** The gelateria may not be sufficiently engaged in researching new ingredients and innovative processes.
   - **Possible Improvement:** Invest in continuous research to stay at the forefront of sustainable trends and innovation in the industry.

8. **Effective Eco-Marketing:**
   - **Weakness:** Marketing strategies may not be fully aligned with sustainable goals.
   - **Possible Improvement:** Review and optimize marketing strategies to ensure they fully reflect the gelateria's commitment to sustainability.

9. **Environmental Impact Monitoring:**
   - **Weakness:** The monitoring system may not be detailed enough to fully assess the environmental impact of sustainable practices.
   - **Possible Improvement:** Implement more advanced environmental impact monitoring systems for more detailed and informative data.

Addressing these weaknesses can further empower the gelateria's commitment to sustainability, enhancing the consistency and effectiveness of eco-friendly practices.

Examples and Case Studies: Chapter 11: Sustainability

Examples and Case Studies:

1. **Responsible Ingredient Sourcing:**

   - **Example:** "NaturaGusto" gelateria has collaborated with small local producers, promoting sustainable agriculture and reducing the supply chain. This choice not only supports the local economy but also ensures fresh and high-quality ingredients.

2. **Energy Efficiency and Waste Reduction:**

   - **Example:** "EcoGelato" implemented a residual energy recycling system from the ice cream production process, significantly reducing overall energy consumption. Additionally, they developed partnerships with local farmers to repurpose by-products as animal feed, minimizing waste.

3. **Active Community Engagement:**

   - **Example:** "GreenScoop" organizes monthly workshops in collaboration with local schools to educate students about sustainable practices. This engagement not only fosters environmental awareness but also creates a sense of community involvement.

4. **Transparent Communication:**

   - **Example:** "ClearFlavors" gelateria openly communicates the challenges faced in transitioning to sustainable practices. By sharing their journey, they build trust with customers and create a more authentic connection with their audience.

5. **Environmental Certifications and Transparency:**

   - **Example:** "EcoCertifiedTreats" proudly displays their environmental certifications, assuring customers of their commitment to sustainable practices. This transparency builds credibility and attracts environmentally conscious consumers.

6. **Employee Education:**

   - **Example:** "GreenTeamGelato" conducts regular training sessions for staff on the importance of sustainability. This not only empowers employees to actively participate in eco-friendly initiatives but also enhances the overall team commitment to green practices.

7. **Research and Innovation:**

   - **Example:** "InnovateScoops" consistently invests in research to discover new ingredients with lower environmental impact. By staying ahead of industry trends, they continuously offer innovative and sustainable options to their customers.

8. **Effective Eco-Marketing:**

- **Example:** "EcoChillGelato" integrates sustainability into their marketing campaigns, emphasizing the eco-friendly choices available to customers. This approach not only attracts environmentally conscious consumers but also educates a broader audience about sustainable options.

9. **Environmental Impact Monitoring:**

   - **Example:** "EcoMetricsGelato" employs advanced monitoring systems to assess the environmental impact of their practices. By regularly analyzing data, they make informed decisions to further minimize their ecological footprint.

These examples and case studies provide real-world illustrations of successful sustainability practices in gelaterias, offering valuable insights and inspiration for the implementation of similar initiatives.

Your Thoughts and Next Steps: Chapter 11: Sustainability

Your Thoughts:

1. **Responsible Ingredient Sourcing:**

   - **Thoughts:** Diversifying the supplier base is crucial for long-term stability and inclusivity. Consider exploring partnerships with small local producers to enhance sustainability and promote diversity.

2. **Energy Efficiency and Waste Reduction:**

   - **Thoughts:** Conduct a thorough analysis of production processes to identify additional opportunities for energy efficiency and waste reduction. Regularly monitor and optimize processes for maximum efficiency.

3. **Active Community Engagement:**

   - **Thoughts:** Building targeted engagement initiatives for specific demographic groups in the community can further enhance the gelateria's impact. Consider collaborating with local schools or specific interest groups.

4. **Transparent Communication:**

   - **Thoughts:** Openly sharing challenges faced in the pursuit of sustainability is a commendable approach. Continue to communicate transparently with customers, emphasizing the commitment to overcoming challenges.

5. **Environmental Certifications and Transparency:**

   - **Thoughts:** Research and obtain recognized environmental certifications to strengthen the gelateria's credibility in the eyes of environmentally conscious consumers.

6. **Employee Education:**

   - **Thoughts:** Periodic training programs for staff are essential to ensure everyone is aligned with the importance of sustainability. Actively involve employees in eco-friendly initiatives to foster a sense of shared commitment.

7. **Research and Innovation:**

   - **Thoughts:** Investing in continuous research is key to staying at the forefront of sustainable trends and innovation. Explore new ingredients and processes to maintain a competitive edge in the industry.

8. **Effective Eco-Marketing:**

   - **Thoughts:** Regularly review and optimize marketing strategies to ensure they align seamlessly with the gelateria's sustainable goals. Effective eco-marketing can play a crucial role in attracting and retaining environmentally conscious customers.

9. **Environmental Impact Monitoring:**

   - **Thoughts:** Implement more advanced environmental impact monitoring systems to gather detailed data on the ecological footprint. This information can guide informed decision-making and further enhance sustainability.

Next Steps:

1. **Responsible Ingredient Sourcing:**

   - **Action:** Initiate discussions with local small producers to explore potential partnerships. Consider creating a diverse network of suppliers to enhance sustainability and support local businesses.

2. **Energy Efficiency and Waste Reduction:**

   - **Action:** Conduct a detailed analysis of current production processes to identify specific areas for improvement in energy efficiency and waste reduction. Implement changes based on the findings to optimize overall sustainability.

3. **Active Community Engagement:**

   - **Action:** Identify specific interest groups in the community and create targeted engagement initiatives. Explore collaboration opportunities with local schools or community organizations to expand the gelateria's impact.

4. **Transparent Communication:**

   - **Action:** Continue to communicate transparently with customers, sharing both successes and challenges in the journey toward sustainability. Consider creating visually engaging materials to highlight sustainable practices during customer visits.

5. **Environmental Certifications and Transparency:**

- **Action:** Research and identify respected environmental certifications relevant to the gelateria's practices. Work toward obtaining these certifications and prominently display them to build trust with environmentally conscious consumers.

6. **Employee Education:**

- **Action:** Implement periodic training programs for staff on the importance of sustainability. Actively involve employees in eco-friendly initiatives to foster a sense of shared commitment to green practices.

7. **Research and Innovation:**

- **Action:** Allocate resources to ongoing research on new ingredients and innovative processes. Stay informed about industry trends to consistently offer innovative and sustainable options to customers.

8. **Effective Eco-Marketing:**

- **Action:** Regularly review and optimize marketing strategies to ensure they effectively communicate the gelateria's commitment to sustainability. Consider incorporating customer incentives for adopting eco-friendly practices.

9. **Environmental Impact Monitoring:**

- **Action:** Implement more advanced environmental impact monitoring systems to gather detailed data on the gelateria's ecological footprint. Use this information to make informed decisions and continuously improve sustainability practices.

These next steps aim to guide the gelateria toward further strengthening its commitment to sustainability and ensuring a consistent and impactful eco-friendly approach

Chapter 12: The Personal Touch in the Gelateria

"The Personal Touch" is what makes a gelateria truly unique and memorable for customers. Here, we will explore how to add a distinctive touch to your gelateria, creating an experience that goes beyond the simple consumption of ice cream.

1. **Welcoming Design:**

- Warm and Inviting Atmosphere: Invest in interior design that conveys a welcoming atmosphere. Use warm colors, soft lighting, and comfortable furnishings to create an environment that invites customers to relax and enjoy their ice cream.

2. **Service Personalization:**

- Personal Interaction: Encourage staff to interact personally with customers. Know their names, listen to their preferences, and create a personalized experience. Friendly and attentive service can make a difference.

3. **Unique and Artisanal Flavors:**

- Exclusive Creations: Offer unique and artisanal ice cream flavors that cannot be found elsewhere. Experiment with local and innovative ingredients to create a menu that reflects your creativity and love for the art of ice cream.

4. **Stories Behind the Flavors:**

- Engaging Narrative: Tell stories behind each flavor. Give customers a narrative experience, explaining the inspiration behind each creation and involving them in the gelateria's story.

5. **Cultural and Artistic Events:**

- Cultural Expression: Organize cultural and artistic events in the gelateria. Local art exhibitions, musical performances, or themed nights can create a vibrant and engaging atmosphere.

6. **Evolving Menu:**

- Regular Rotation: Update the menu regularly with new seasonal flavors and special creations. This will keep customers interested and invite them to come back to discover the latest innovations.

7. **Community Participation:**

- Active Engagement: Actively participate in community events. Sponsor local teams, participate in fairs, or contribute to charitable causes. Community engagement creates a stronger bond with customers.

8. **Interactive Experiences:**

- Gelato Workshops: Organize gelato workshops where customers can learn to create their own ice cream. These interactive experiences increase customer engagement and loyalty.

9. **Personalized Loyalty Programs:**

- Exclusive Benefits: Create loyalty programs that offer personalized benefits. For example, offer discounts or special flavors based on customers' preferred tastes.

10. Curiosity and Entertainment:

- Connoisseur's Corner: Create a connoisseur's corner where customers can learn interesting facts about ice cream, the history of ingredients, or traditions related to certain flavors.

This chapter will highlight how the "Personal Touch" contributes to creating a unique experience for customers, going beyond a simple commercial transaction and creating a lasting connection.

Strengths and Areas for Improvement: Chapter 12: The Personal Touch

Chapter 12: The Personal Touch in the Gelateria - Strengths and Areas for Improvement

1. Strengths:

- Personalized Service: Your commitment to providing personalized and friendly service is a strength. Knowing customers by name and listening to their preferences contributes to creating a welcoming experience.

- Unique and Artisanal Flavors: Offering unique and artisanal ice cream flavors is a distinctive element. Continue experimenting with local ingredients and introducing new creations to maintain customer interest.

- Community Engagement: Active participation in community events is a strength that creates a stronger bond with customers. Involvement in charitable causes and local sponsorships is a positive way to contribute to the community.

- Interactive Experiences: Events like gelato workshops and other interactive experiences add a special touch. These initiatives can increase engagement and create lasting memories.

2. Areas for Improvement:

- Communication of Flavor Stories: You could improve the communication of stories behind ice cream flavors. Create engaging narratives that emotionally connect customers with your creations, turning ice cream into a more meaningful experience.

- Menu Rotation: Evaluate the frequency of menu rotation. Ensure a balance between regular updates and the availability of customer-favorite options. Find a balance between innovation and continuity.

- Personalized Loyalty Programs: Explore options to make loyalty programs even more personalized. You could implement a system that automatically tracks customer preferences and offers more targeted benefits.

- Cultural and Artistic Experiences: Deepen cultural and artistic experiences organized in the gelateria. You could develop further collaborations with local artists or explore more in-depth cultural themes to enrich the atmosphere.

- Innovation in Welcoming: Continue to innovate in the welcoming aspect of the gelateria. Consider elements such as eco-friendly design, artistic installations, or seasonal settings to create an visually appealing experience.

- Customer Feedback: Implement a structured system to collect customer feedback. This could provide valuable insights on how to further improve service and better meet customer expectations.

These suggestions can help consolidate existing strengths and further refine the approach to the "Personal Touch" in the gelateria.

Chapter 12: The Personal Touch in the Gelateria - Weak Points and Mistakes to Avoid

1. **Ineffective Communication of Flavor Stories:**

   - Weak Point: Ineffective communication of the stories behind flavors may reduce the opportunity to create emotional connections with customers.

   - Solution: Develop a more engaging narrative approach, perhaps using visual elements or emotional details to make the stories more memorable.

2. **Balancing Innovation and Continuity:**

   - Weak Point: Excessively frequent menu rotation may lead to the loss of customer-favorite options, while a lack of innovation may make the experience less exciting.

   - Solution: Find a balanced middle ground between regular menu updates and maintaining beloved options. Monitor customer preferences and respond accordingly.

3. **Suboptimal Personalized Loyalty Programs:**

   - Weak Point: Loyalty programs may not be optimized to offer truly personalized and targeted benefits.

   - Solution: Implement a more advanced system that automatically tracks customer preferences and provides personalized benefits based on their purchasing behavior.

4. **Insufficiently In-Depth Cultural and Artistic Experiences:**

   - Weak Point: Cultural and artistic experiences may not be sufficiently in-depth to create a significant impact.

   - Solution: Deepen collaborations with local artists and expand cultural experiences to offer a richer and more engaging atmosphere.

5. **Lack of Innovation in Welcoming:**
   - Weak Point: The lack of innovation in the welcoming aspect may reduce the visual appeal of the gelateria.
   - Solution: Explore new design elements, artistic installations, or seasonal settings to maintain a visually captivating environment.

6. **Lack of Structured Customer Feedback:**
   - Weak Point: The lack of a structured system to collect customer feedback may reduce the ability to make improvements based on real opinions.
   - Solution: Implement a structured feedback system, perhaps through online surveys or comment cards in the gelateria, to obtain detailed input.

Avoiding these mistakes and addressing weak points can significantly improve the effectiveness of the "Personal Touch" in your gelateria, creating a more memorable and satisfying experience for customers.

Chapter 12: The Personal Touch in the Gelateria - Examples and Case Studies

Chapter 12: The Personal Touch in the Gelateria - Examples and Case Studies

1. **Effective Communication of Flavor Stories:**
   - Example: A gelateria tells exciting stories about the origins of its ingredients. For instance, strawberry ice cream might be associated with a small local farm, showcasing images of the cultivation and harvesting process.

2. **Balancing Innovation and Continuity:**
   - Example: A gelateria introduces new seasonal flavors periodically but maintains a "Classic Menu" with customer favorites. Innovation merges with continuity, satisfying both those seeking something new and those desiring classics.

3. **Personalized Loyalty Programs:**
   - Example: A loyalty program automatically records customer preferences. Those who frequently purchase fruit flavors might receive special offers on new fruity creations, while chocolate lovers receive benefits on related flavors.

4. **Cultural and Artistic Experiences:**
   - Example: A gelateria organizes monthly art exhibitions featuring local artists, turning the space into a temporary gallery. Each month, ice cream is inspired by exhibited artworks, creating a multisensory experience.

5. **Innovation in Welcoming:**

- Example: A gelateria creates a special tasting area where customers can experience new flavors before choosing. The area is decorated with innovative and interactive elements, adding visual charm to the experience.

6. **Structured Customer Feedback:**

- Example: The gelateria uses feedback cards distributed at tables and online through the website. It seeks specific opinions on ice cream quality and service, offering incentives to encourage customers to share their thoughts.

These case studies demonstrate how implementing personalized and innovative strategies can enrich the "Personal Touch" in a gelateria, making it a unique and engaging place for customers.

Chapter 12: The Personal Touch in the Gelateria - Future and Perspectives

Chapter 12: The Personal Touch in the Gelateria - Future and Perspectives

The future of the "Personal Touch" in the gelateria looks exciting, with a continuous shift towards increasingly personalized and engaging experiences. Here are some key perspectives:

1. **Technology for Personalization:**

- Future Scenario: Advanced technologies like artificial intelligence and data analysis will be employed to anticipate customer preferences. Gelaterias could offer personalized suggestions based on purchase history and individual preferences.

2. **Virtual and Augmented Reality Experiences:**

- Future Scenario: Virtual and augmented reality experiences could transform the gelateria visit. Customers might engage in virtual tours of ingredient production farms or customize their ice cream through apps and wearable devices.

3. **Sustainability as a Central Element:**

- Future Scenario: Sustainability will become a central element of the "Personal Touch." Gelaterias could communicate their eco-friendly practices more deeply, involving customers in sustainable initiatives and promoting environmental awareness.

4. **Collaborations with Artists and Creatives:**

- Future Scenario: Gelaterias could intensify collaborations with artists and creatives, turning spaces into actual works of art. Cultural events and temporary art exhibitions could become an integral part of the customer experience.

5. **Integration with the Wellness Concept:**

- Future Scenario: The idea of wellness could integrate more into flavor creation. Functional ice creams, enriched with healthy ingredients and suitable for specific dietary needs, could become a prominent trend.

6. **Active Community Engagement:**

- Future Scenario: Active community engagement could grow, with gelaterias serving as local cultural centers. Events, workshops, and volunteer initiatives could become an integral part of gelateria missions.

7. **Advanced Sensory Experiences:**

- Future Scenario: Sensory experiences could further evolve. Gelaterias might experiment with customized aromas, innovative visual presentations, and ambient sounds to create a unique multisensory experience.

8. **Care for Visual and Architectural Environment:**

- Future Scenario: Care for the visual and architectural environment of gelaterias could receive more attention. Ecological designs, sustainable materials, and captivating aesthetics could become integral to the "Personal Touch" strategy.

9. **Continuous Customer Education:**

- Future Scenario: Gelaterias could take a more active role in educating customers about the production process, ingredient origins, and the impact of their choices. Interactive workshops and educational materials could become more widespread.

10. **Virtual Connection with Producers and Suppliers:**

- Future Scenario: Gelaterias could develop closer connections with ingredient producers and suppliers. Sharing stories and direct information from the source could strengthen the bond between customers and the entire production chain.

These perspectives reflect a future where personalization, sustainability, and innovation continue to define the "Personal Touch" in the gelateria, discussing further possibilities.

Chapter 12: The Personal Touch in the Gelateria - Memorable Events

Chapter 12: The Personal Touch in the Gelateria - Memorable Events

Events in your gelateria are a unique opportunity to create unforgettable experiences for customers. Here are some ideas to make events an integral part of the "Personal Touch":

1. **Surprise Themed Evenings:**

- Organize surprise evenings with unique themes. It could be an evening inspired by a movie, a season, or a specific culture. Mystery and anticipation create a special atmosphere.

2. **Gelato and Live Music:**

   - Collaborate with local musicians for evenings of gelato and live music. Create a relaxed atmosphere where customers can enjoy their favorite ice cream while listening to live performances.

3. **Flavor Creation Competitions:**

   - Invite customers to participate in flavor creation competitions. The most original ideas could become special flavors on the menu. Involving the community creates a sense of belonging.

4. **Guided Tasting Events:**

   - Organize guided tasting sessions where customers can explore different flavor combinations. Guide participants through a sensory journey, explaining the art of pairing flavors.

5. **Gelato & Art:**

   - Collaborate with local artists to organize art creation events in the gelateria. Customers can enjoy ice cream while participating in artistic workshops or admiring exhibited artworks.

6. **Stars and Flavors Night:**

   - Organize a "Stars and Flavors Night" where customers can enjoy ice cream under **the starry sky. Add romantic elements like soft lights and thematic decorations.**

7. **Gelato and Book Club:**

   - Create a book club in the gelateria. Enthusiasts can meet to discuss books while savoring special flavors inspired by the stories. An opportunity to combine two of your passions.

8. **Moving Gelato:**

   - Organize mobile events in different community locations. A gelato cart in a park or at a local market can attract new customers and bring your personal touch to different places.

9. **Gelato for Charitable Causes:**

   - Dedicate one day a month to raising funds for local charitable causes. Part of the proceeds from ice cream sales could be donated to non-profit organizations.

10. **Outdoor Yoga and Gelato:**

    - Organize an outdoor yoga session followed by a gelato tasting. Combine wellness and indulgence, creating a unique event.

Each event should reflect the personality of your gelateria and your mission of inclusion and connection with the community.

Chapter 13: Events and Collaborations - A World of Opportunities

Events and collaborations are an extraordinary means to engage the community and give your gelateria a unique character. In this chapter, we will explore how to plan memorable events and create meaningful collaborations. Here are some suggestions:

1. **Monthly Event Series:**

   - Organize a series of thematic monthly events. For example, a "Movie and Gelato Night" or a "Seasonal Celebration." This creates anticipation and engages the community continuously.

2. **Collaborations with Other Local Businesses:**

   - Collaborate with other local businesses for joint events. For instance, a gelato tasting at a local bookstore or a collaboration with a café to create special flavors.

3. **Charity Events and Volunteering:**

   - Organize charity events and volunteer days. Involve the community in your solidarity mission, doing good while promoting your gelateria.

4. **Artisan Gelato Festival:**

   - Create an artisan gelato festival, involving other local gelaterias. This not only promotes the art of gelato but also collaboration between local businesses.

5. **Cultural Nights:**

   - Dedicate evenings to specific cultures with gelato flavors and activities related to that culture. It could be an Italian night with gelati inspired by the Italian tradition, considering your passion for optometry.

6. **Tasting Events with Experts:**

   - Invite industry experts for tasting events. It could be a chocolate expert for a chocolate-gelato pairing night or a local farmer to talk about ingredients.

7. **Artistic-Culinary Collaborations:**

- Collaborate with local artists to create artistic culinary experiences. For example, an artist could create artwork inspired by your gelato flavors.

8. **Gelato Competitions for the Community:**

   - Organize gelato competitions open to the community. This involves people in the creative process and can lead to new ideas for innovative flavors.

9. **Educational Events for Children:**

   - Plan educational events for children. Gelato workshops where the youngest can learn to make their gelato are both fun and educational.

10. **Local Music Nights:**

   - Collaborate with local musicians for music nights in the gelateria. This creates a lively atmosphere and attracts a variety of audiences.

The goal is to create events that are more than just gelato tastings but genuine experiences for the community.

Strengths and Areas for Improvement: Chapter 13: Events and Collaborations

Chapter 13: Events and Collaborations - Strengths and Areas for Improvement

1. **Strengths:**

   - Variety and Originality of Events: Your gelateria excels in creating various and original events, offering the community a wide range of experiences.

   - Community Engagement: You have demonstrated strong community engagement through charity events and volunteer initiatives, creating a closer bond with customers.

   - Collaborations with Other Local Businesses: Collaborations with other local businesses are a strength that can lead to lasting partnerships and mutual support.

   - Focus on Themed Events: The focus on themed events provides variety and uniqueness, attracting a diversified audience interested in specific experiences.

2. **Areas for Improvement:**

   - Measurement of Event Impact: Implementing systems to measure the effectiveness and impact of events on customer and gelateria visibility could be beneficial.

   - Expansion of Collaborations: Explore opportunities to expand collaborations with other local businesses, exploring new sectors and deepening existing relationships.

   - Online Engagement: Strengthen online engagement, using digital platforms to promote events and engage a broader audience, even beyond your local area.

- Post-Event Feedback: Collect post-event feedback to assess participant satisfaction and identify areas for improvement or new ideas.

- More Structured Educational Events: For children's educational events, consider creating more structured and educational programs, perhaps in collaboration with local schools.

- Sustainability in Events: Integrate sustainable practices into events, reducing waste and promoting environmental awareness.

- Involvement of Local Artists: Deepen the involvement of local artists in collaborations, creating a stronger bridge between art and taste in your gelateria.

- Promotion Before Events: It might be helpful to intensify promotional efforts before events, creating anticipation and attracting a wider audience.

- Variation of Event Timings: Explore the possibility of varying event timings to make experiences accessible at different times and to a broader audience.

These considerations could help optimize the planning and execution of events and collaborations, amplifying their positive impact on your gelateria

Weaknesses and Mistakes to Avoid: Chapter 13: Events and Collaborations

1. **Weaknesses:**

   - **Lack of Post-Event Evaluation:** Not collecting post-event feedback could limit your understanding of the effectiveness of events and areas for improvement.

   - **Limited Online Engagement:** If online engagement is still limited, there might be an opportunity to reach a broader audience through more robust digital strategies.

   - **Sustainability in Events:** The integration of sustainable practices in events could be improved to reduce the overall environmental impact of activities.

   - **Pre-Event Promotion:** If pre-event promotion is limited, it might affect participation and community awareness of initiatives.

2. **Mistakes to Avoid:**

   - **Inadequate Timing Planning for Events:** Avoid planning events at non-ideal times for your community or when there are other local events that could divert attention.

   - **Irrelevant Collaborations:** Avoid collaborations that may not be relevant to your gelateria or fail to spark interest in your community.

- **Lack of a Clear Impact Measurement Strategy:** Avoid not having a clear strategy to measure the effectiveness and impact of events, limiting the ability to assess success.

- **Excessive Complexity in Organization:** Avoid making events and collaborations overly complex. Complicated organization could lead to stress and might not be fully understood by the community.

- **Absence of an Error Management Plan:** Avoid not having an error management plan. Be prepared for contingencies and ensure that staff is promptly trained to handle unexpected situations.

- **Last-Minute Promotional Efforts:** Avoid relying on last-minute promotional efforts. Early promotion is crucial to attract a larger number of participants.

- **Lack of Active Online Engagement:** Avoid not actively engaging the community online. Use social media and other digital channels to create anticipation and engage a broader audience.

Addressing these weaknesses and avoiding mistakes can contribute to improving the planning and execution of events and collaborations, making each initiative more effective and satisfying.

Examples and Case Studies: Chapter 13: Events and Collaborations

1. **Collaboration with Local Bookstore:**

   - **Objective:** Promote the love for reading and gelato.

   - **Execution:** Collaboration with a local bookstore for a "Gelato & Books" evening. Creation of flavors inspired by beloved books. Reading sessions and discussions on the book of the month.

- **Result:** Increased visits to the bookstore and gelateria, creating a cultural atmosphere where people can enjoy books and gelato.

2. **Artisan Gelato Festival:**
   - **Objective:** Celebrate the art of gelato and involve other local gelaterias.
   - **Execution:** Organization of an "Artisan Gelato Festival" in collaboration with various local gelaterias. Each gelateria presents unique flavors and participates in friendly competitions.
   - **Result:** Increased interest in artisan gelato in the community. Increased sales for all participating gelaterias.

3. **Charity Event with Environmental Association:**
   - **Objective:** Promote sustainability and raise funds for an environmental association.
   - **Execution:** Organization of a charity event "Gelato for Nature." Presentation of flavors with sustainable ingredients. A percentage of sales donated to the association.
   - **Result:** Community engagement in sustainable practices and significant fundraising.

4. **Collaboration with Local Artist:**
   - **Objective:** Unite art and gelato to create a unique experience.
   - **Execution:** Collaboration with a local artist to create an edible artwork using gelato and toppings. The artwork is displayed in the gelateria.
   - **Result:** Increased interest in both art and gelato. Visits from enthusiasts of both disciplines.

5. **Creative Gelato Competition:**
   - **Objective:** Involve the community in creating innovative flavors.
   - **Execution:** Organization of a "Creative Gelato Competition" open to the community. The best ideas become special menu flavors for a month.
   - **Result:** Enthusiastic community participation, with new ideas becoming a sales success.

6. **Night of Stars and Flavors:**
   - **Objective:** Create a romantic experience under the starry sky.
   - **Execution:** Special evening with thematic decorations, soft lights, and gelato inspired by the night sky. Outdoor tables for enjoying gelato under the stars.

- **Result:** Romantic atmosphere, attraction of couples, and success on social media.

These examples demonstrate how events and collaborations can be diversified and adapted to your vision of community inclusion and engagement.

Future and Perspectives: Chapter 13: Events and Collaborations

Looking to the future of events and collaborations for your gelateria is crucial to maintaining community interest and relevance over time. Here are some perspectives and suggestions for the next chapter:

1. **Development of Successful Recurring Events:**
   - Identify events that have been most successful and consider making them recurring. Annual or monthly events can become fixed appointments in your community's routine.

2. **Exploration of New Themes and Collaborations:**
   - Continue to explore new themes for events and seek innovative collaborations. Keep your customers curious by offering ever-changing experiences.

3. **Active Online Engagement:**
   - Boost online engagement through social media and other digital channels. Use these tools to preview events, engage the community, and collect post-event feedback.

4. **Sustainability as a Key Element:**
   - Deepen the integration of sustainable practices in events. Demonstrate your commitment to environmental sustainability, reflecting your gelateria's values.

5. **Long-Term Partnerships:**

- Explore long-term partnerships with other local businesses. Continuous collaboration can lead to a stronger network and mutual support in the long run.

6. **Involvement of Local Artists and Creatives:**

   - Continue to involve local artists and creatives in collaborations. This not only adds a unique touch to events but also supports the local creative scene.

7. **Expansion of Educational Offerings:**

   - Expand educational events by offering more structured and engaging workshops. Involve local schools to create educational programs on artisanal gelato production.

8. **Globalization of Flavors:**

   - Explore the possibility of introducing flavors inspired by international cuisines. This can broaden the appeal of your gelateria, reflecting your vision of inclusion.

9. **Participation in External Events:**

   - Consider participating in external events, such as food fairs or local festivals. This exposure can attract new customers and broaden the visibility of your gelateria.

10. **Adaptation to Market Trends:**

    - Stay updated on food industry trends and adjust events accordingly. Being in tune with what the audience is looking for can keep your gelateria in step with the times.

Looking ahead with enthusiasm and flexibility is essential to ensure that your gelateria continues to thrive in the evolving needs of the community.

Events, Fairs, and Courses - A World of Opportunities for Your Gelateria

1. **Participation in Food Fairs:**

- **Objective:** Increase gelateria visibility.

- **Execution:** Participation in local or national food fairs. Presentation of special flavors, gelato preparation demonstrations, and distribution of free samples.

- **Result:** Expanded customer base and networking opportunities with other food industry operators.

2. **Organization of Monthly Themed Events:**

- **Objective:** Maintain continuous community interest.

- **Execution:** Organization of monthly themed events such as tasting nights, cultural evenings, or live music nights.

- **Result:** Customer loyalty and creation of fixed appointments in the community calendar.

3. **Gelato Competitions and Contests:**

- **Objective:** Showcase the creativity of your gelateria.

- **Execution:** Participation in gelato competitions or organization of internal contests. Involve the community in voting for the best flavor.

- **Result:** Increased notoriety and demonstration of your expertise in the industry.

4. **Artisan Gelato Courses:**

- **Objective:** Share your knowledge and expertise.

- **Execution:** Organization of artisan gelato courses open to the public. Cover topics such as gelato preparation, ingredient management, and service techniques.

- **Result:** Building a closer bond with the community, active engagement, and sharing of experiences.

5. **Collaborations with Other Gelaterias:**

- **Objective:** Promote collaboration and diversity in the industry.

- **Execution:** Collaborations with other local gelaterias for joint events, such as gelato tastings and exchange of experiences.

- **Result:** Reinforcement of solidarity among gelaterias and promotion of the local gelato ecosystem.

6. **Participation in Charity Events:**

- **Objective:** Demonstrate social commitment.

- **Execution:** Involvement in charity events, such as fundraising or volunteer service in collaboration with local organizations.
- **Result:** Building a positive reputation and active contribution to the community.

7. **Events on Sustainability:**
   - **Objective:** Promote environmental sustainability.
   - **Execution:** Organization of events focused on sustainability, such as evenings dedicated to eco-friendly flavors or initiatives to reduce waste.
   - **Result:** Demonstration of commitment to environmental issues and community engagement.

8. **Participation in Industry Conferences:**
   - **Objective:** Stay updated on trends and connect with industry experts.
   - **Execution:** Participation in gelato industry conferences, networking events, and training sessions.
   - **Result:** Continuous learning, expanding knowledge, and opportunities for future collaborations.

9. **Guided Tasting Nights:**
   - **Objective:** Educate customers' palates.
   - **Execution:** Organization of guided tasting nights with a focus on specific flavors, pairings with wines, or desserts.
   - **Result:** Enhancement of the customer experience and broadening understanding of flavors.

10. **Mobile Gelato Unit:**
    - **Objective:** Bring gelato directly to the community.
    - **Execution:** Organization of a cart or mobile van to serve gelato in different areas of your city or at local events.
    - **Result:** Increased sales and maximization of visibility.

Exploring these opportunities can open new avenues for your gelateria, offering a variety of experiences to the community and solidifying your position in the industry

Chapter 14: Challenges and Solutions - Weaknesses and Pitfalls to Avoid

1. Weaknesses:

   - Inventory Management: The current weakness could be inventory management. Identify specific areas where difficulties exist and work on concrete strategies to reduce waste and improve efficiency in ingredient management.

   - Internal Communication: If there are challenges in internal communication, this could affect team cohesion and service quality. Strive to improve transparency and clarity in internal communications.

   - Reactivity to Industry Trends: A weakness might be reactivity to industry trends. Ensure you are constantly updated on the latest innovations and find ways to adapt your gelateria to these trends promptly.

   - Community Engagement: If there is room for improvement in community engagement, consider more active strategies to gather feedback and involve customers in key gelateria decisions.

2. **Pitfalls to Avoid:**

   - Underestimating the Importance of Training: Avoid underestimating the importance of continuous staff training. Ensure all team members are well-trained to perform different tasks during peak periods.

   - Unpreparedness for Emergencies: Avoid being inadequately prepared for emergencies such as equipment breakdowns or other unforeseen events. A robust emergency management plan can make a difference during critical moments.

   - Ineffective Event Promotion: Do not neglect effective event promotion. Effective communication is crucial to maximize participation. Be proactive in using online and offline channels to make events known to the community.

   - Lack of Diversification of Educational Offerings: Avoid insufficient diversification of educational offerings. Explore opportunities to introduce more in-depth and engaging workshops to satisfy a clientele eager to learn.

   - Failure to Adapt to Customer Preferences: Do not neglect changing customer preferences. Collect feedback regularly and experiment with new flavors to meet evolving customer needs.

   - Lack of Industry Trend Monitoring: Avoid not carefully monitoring industry trends. Indifference to new innovations could compromise the competitiveness of the gelateria.

Addressing these weaknesses and avoiding pitfalls can contribute to strengthening your gelateria and improving customer satisfaction.

Chapter 14: Challenges and Solutions - Examples and Case Studies

1. **Inventory Management:**

   - *Challenge:* A gelateria struggled with inefficient inventory management, leading to frequent ingredient wastage.

   - *Solution:* Implemented a more precise stock rotation and an ingredient expiration monitoring system.

   - *Result:* Significant reduction in waste and improved inventory management.

2. **Internal Communication:**

   - *Challenge:* Another gelateria faced internal communication issues, causing misunderstandings among staff.

   - *Solution:* Introduced an online internal communication platform for real-time information sharing.

   - *Result:* Improved transparency and reduced misunderstandings among staff.

3. **Reactivity to Industry Trends:**

   - *Challenge:* A gelateria was losing opportunities to capitalize on new industry trends.

   - *Solution:* Established a research and development team to monitor industry trends and experiment with new flavors.

   - *Result:* Timely introduction of new products, keeping the gelateria in line with customer expectations.

4. **Community Engagement:**

   - *Challenge:* A gelateria aimed to strengthen community ties but struggled to actively engage customers.

   - *Solution:* Launched an online campaign to gather suggestions for new flavors and events.

   - *Result:* Increased customer interest and greater involvement in the gelateria's activities.

5. **Continuous Staff Training:**

   - *Challenge:* A gelateria had an inflexible team, with members unable to adapt to different tasks.

- *Solution:* Implemented a continuous training program allowing staff to acquire versatile skills.

- *Result:* Greater flexibility during peak periods and a more cohesive team.

6. **Emergency Management:**

    - *Challenge:* A gelateria was inadequately prepared for emergencies such as equipment breakdowns.

    - *Solution:* Created an emergency checklist with clear procedures for sudden breakdowns.

    - *Result:* Improved preparedness and reduced impact during critical situations.

7. **Effective Event Promotion:**

    - *Challenge:* A gelateria organized events but struggled to maximize participation.

    - *Solution:* Collaborated with local influencers for event promotion and used targeted online ads.

    - *Result:* Increased participation and greater online visibility.

8. **Diversification of Educational Offerings:**

    - *Challenge:* A gelateria wanted to expand educational offerings but faced difficulty engaging customers.

    - *Solution:* Introduced more in-depth and engaging workshops, promoted through online channels.

    - *Result:* Increased participation in courses and greater interest in educational activities.

9. **Monitoring Industry Trends:**

    - *Challenge:* A gelateria was not paying enough attention to new industry trends.

    - *Solution:* Designated a trends manager, participated in industry fairs, and regularly read specialized publications.

    - *Result:* Timely introduction of new products in response to evolving customer expectations.

Addressing these challenges with targeted solutions has led to significant improvements for various gelaterias

Chapter 15: Collection of Italian Gelato Recipes

1. **Stracciatella Gelato:**

   - *Ingredients:* Whole milk, cream, sugar, dark chocolate.
   - *Procedure:* Prepare a gelato base with milk, cream, and sugar. During the final freezing phase, add melted dark chocolate in a thin stream to create elegant chocolate stripes in the gelato.

2. **Sicilian Pistachio:**

   - *Ingredients:* Bronte pistachios, milk, cream, sugar.
   - *Procedure:* Finely chop the pistachios and mix them with the gelato base. The Bronte pistachio variety imparts a rich and authentic flavor to this gelato.

3. **Tiramisu Gelato:**

   - *Ingredients:* Mascarpone, eggs, sugar, coffee, ladyfingers.
   - *Procedure:* Prepare a tiramisu cream with mascarpone, eggs, and sugar. Add cooled strong coffee. During the final freezing phase, incorporate pieces of ladyfingers previously soaked in coffee.

4. **Lemon Sorbet:**

   - *Ingredients:* Lemon juice, water, sugar.
   - *Procedure:* Mix lemon juice with water and sugar until obtaining a homogeneous mixture. Freeze using the sorbet technique for a refreshing lemon gelato.

5. **Dark Chocolate and Orange:**

   - *Ingredients:* Dark chocolate, orange zest, milk, cream, sugar.
   - *Procedure:* Melt the dark chocolate and mix it with the gelato base. Add grated orange zest for a fresh and aromatic touch.

6. **Fior di Latte Gelato:**

   - *Ingredients:* Fresh milk, cream, sugar.
   - *Procedure:* Use high-quality ingredients to highlight the sweet and creamy flavor of milk. A simple base that celebrates freshness.

7. **Amarena Cherry Gelato:**

   - *Ingredients:* Amarena cherries, sugar, water.

- *Procedure:* Create a syrup with Amarena cherries and water. Add this syrup to the gelato base for a fruity and slightly acidic flavor.

8. **Bourbon Vanilla:**

   - *Ingredients:* Bourbon vanilla beans, milk, cream, sugar.

   - *Procedure:* Scrape the seeds from Bourbon vanilla beans and mix them with the gelato base. This imparts an intense and aromatic aroma.

9. **White Chocolate and Raspberry Gelato:**

   - *Ingredients:* White chocolate, raspberries, milk, cream, sugar.

   - *Procedure:* Melt white chocolate and add it to the gelato base. Add fresh raspberries for a contrast of flavors.

10. **Piedmont Hazelnut:**

    - *Ingredients:* Piedmont hazelnuts, milk, cream, sugar.

    - *Procedure:* Lightly toast the hazelnuts, finely chop them, and mix them with the gelato base. The distinctive flavor of Piedmont hazelnuts will take center stage.

Gelato Base Preparation:

- *Ingredients:*

  - 500 ml whole milk

  - 200 g sugar

  - 6 egg yolks

  - 1 teaspoon vanilla extract (or seeds from one vanilla bean)

- *Instructions:*

  1. Heat the milk in a saucepan over medium heat, just below boiling.

  2. In a separate bowl, whisk egg yolks with sugar until a clear and creamy mixture is obtained.

  3. Slowly pour a small amount of the heated milk into the egg mixture, continuously stirring to temper the yolks and prevent them from cooking.

  4. Pour the egg mixture back into the saucepan with the remaining milk. Continue stirring well.

  5. Return to medium-low heat and cook, stirring constantly, until the mixture slightly thickens. Do not boil.

6.	Remove from heat and let it cool. You can place the bowl in a cold water bath to expedite the cooling process.

7.	Once cooled, add vanilla extract or vanilla bean seeds and mix well.

8.	Cover the bowl with plastic wrap, ensuring it touches the surface of the mixture (preventing the formation of a film), and let it rest in the refrigerator for at least 4-6 hours or preferably overnight.

9.	After the resting period, pour the gelato base into your ice cream maker and follow the manufacturer's instructions to complete the gelato preparation process.

10.	This base can be used as a starting point to create various gelato flavors by adding ingredients like melted chocolate, fruit, nuts, or other elements during the final phase in the ice cream maker. Enjoy preparing and savor your homemade gelato!

Diabetic-friendly Gelato Variant: Vanilla and Almond

- *Ingredients:*
  - 2 cups fresh cream (without added sugars)
  - 1 cup unsweetened almond milk
  - 1/2 cup low-glycemic sweetener (such as stevia or erythritol), or to taste
  - 1 teaspoon vanilla extract
  - A handful of finely chopped almonds (optional, for added crunch)
- *Instructions:*

  1.	In a bowl, mix fresh cream, almond milk, and low-glycemic sweetener.

  2.	Add vanilla extract and mix well to evenly distribute the flavor.

  3.	Taste the mixture and add more sweetener if needed, according to your personal preference.

  4.	Pour the mixture into the ice cream maker and follow the manufacturer's instructions to complete the freezing process.

  5.	If you want to add a crunchy touch, add the chopped almonds during the last phase in the ice cream maker or sprinkle them over the ice cream when serving.

6.   Transfer the gelato to an airtight container and place it in the freezer for at least 4-6 hours to achieve the desired consistency.

7.   This recipe uses low-glycemic sweeteners and almond milk, which is a lighter choice compared to whole milk. However, it's always advisable to consult a health professional, especially when adjusting the diet to manage diabetes. This recipe can be adapted with other low-sugar flavors or ingredients to suit personal tastes.

Experiment with these authentic recipes to create Italian-flavored gelatos that will delight your customers.

Strengths and Areas for Improvement: Chapter 15: Collection of Italian Gelato Recipes

Chapter 15: Collection of Italian Ice Cream Recipes - Strengths and Areas for Improvement

Strengths:

1. **Authenticity of Recipes:**

   - The collection offers authentic recipes rooted in Italian tradition, emphasizing the quality and authenticity of the proposed flavors.

2. **Variety of Flavors:**

   - The diversity of recipes covers a wide range of tastes, from classic dark chocolate to refined Sicilian pistachio, providing a variety that can satisfy different customer preferences.

3. **Use of Quality Ingredients:**

   - The attention to using high-quality ingredients, such as Bronte pistachios or dark chocolate, highlights dedication to quality and authentic taste.

4. **Simplicity and Understandability:**

   - Instructions are clear and understandable, making the recipes accessible even to beginners in artisanal ice cream preparation.

5. **Creativity and Originality:**

   - The inclusion of unusual combinations, like white chocolate and raspberry, shows a creative and original approach that can distinguish the gelateria in the market.

Areas for Improvement:

1. **Inclusion of Healthier Variants:**

   - Consider including lighter or healthier variants in the recipes to cater to an increasingly health-conscious clientele.

2. **Exploration of Innovative Techniques:**

   - Experiment with innovative preparation techniques, such as using nitro ice cream or introducing unusual flavors, to capture the attention of customers.

3. **Promotion of Ingredient Origins:**

   - Add details about the origin of ingredients to emphasize quality and traceability, meeting the growing expectations of an informed clientele.

4. **Community Involvement:**

   - Invite the community to suggest ideas for new flavors or vote on their preferences, fostering not only customer engagement but also inspiring new recipes.

5. **Exploration of Market Trends:**

   - Monitor market trends closely and consider adding popular flavors or ingredients based on public demand.

6. **Creation of a Seasonal Menu:**

   - Introduce a seasonal menu that adapts to temperature changes and holidays, providing new opportunities to attract customers.

7. **Customization of Flavors:**

   - Offer the option to customize some flavors, allowing customers to create their own combinations of ingredients.

8. **Deepening the Story of Each Flavor:**

   - Enrich the chapter with brief stories or anecdotes about the history of each flavor, creating an emotional connection with the products.

Continuing to emphasize quality and authenticity while exploring new ideas and meeting the needs of modern customers can take your gelateria to new levels of success.

Chapter 15: Collection of Italian Ice Cream Recipes - Weaknesses and Mistakes to Avoid

Weaknesses:

1. **Lack of Gluten-Free or Vegan Variants:**

   - Some recipes may not be suitable for customers with dietary restrictions such as gluten or animal products. Integrating gluten-free or vegan variants could expand the audience.

2. **Complexity in Some Recipes:**

- Some recipes might be complex for beginners in artisanal ice cream making. Simplifying instructions or providing alternatives could make the recipes more accessible.

3. **Presence of Hard-to-Find Ingredients:**

   - Using particularly rare or hard-to-find ingredients could limit the practicality of the recipes. Where possible, suggest alternatives or provide tips for online purchasing.

4. **Absence of Low-Sugar Options:**

   - In an era where many customers seek low-sugar options, the absence of specific recipes could be a weakness. Including low-sugar variants could address this growing demand.

Mistakes to Avoid:

1. **Incorrect Ingredient Proportions:**

   - Ensure accurate proportions of ingredients to guarantee the desired consistency and flavor.

2. **Lack of Details on Key Techniques:**

   - Avoid neglecting crucial details about preparation techniques, such as freezing temperature or ingredient incorporation. These details are fundamental to recipe success.

3. **Underestimation of Preparation Times:**

   - Providing accurate preparation times is essential. Underestimating times could lead to frustration and disappointing results for those following the recipes.

4. **Lack of Advice on Specialized Tools:**

   - If a recipe requires the use of specialized tools, make sure to provide alternatives or tips on achieving similar results without expensive equipment.

5. **Omission of Possible Allergens:**

   - Informing about possible allergens in the recipes is crucial for customer safety. Ensure highlighting the presence of common allergens.

6. **Ignoring Market Trends:**

   - Avoid ignoring market trends, as this could limit the potential success of the recipes. Keeping an eye on new trends can inspire new ideas and keep them relevant.

7. **Lack of Presentation Tips:**

- Presentation is crucial in the ice cream world. Providing tips on presenting ice creams attractively can enhance the customer experience.

8. **Omitting Variants for Different Production Sizes:**

   - Omitting variants for different production sizes could limit the adaptability of the recipes to various business needs. Consider variations for small or large productions.

Considering these weaknesses and mistakes to avoid could enhance the completeness and accessibility of your recipe collection.

Chapter 15: Collection of Italian Ice Cream Recipes - Future and Projections

Projections:

1. **Exploration of Healthier Variants:**

   - Introduce healthier variants of the recipes tailored to the needs of an increasingly health-conscious clientele. Include low-sugar, gluten-free, and vegan options.

2. **Collaborations with Local Producers:**

   - Create collaborations with local producers to ensure the supply of fresh and high-quality ingredients. This initiative contributes to sustainability and promotes the local community.

3. **Inclusion of Seasonal and Themed Recipes:**

   - Add a section dedicated to seasonal and themed recipes. This will allow offering customers options more in line with holidays and climate changes.

4. **Video Tutorials and Multimedia Content:**

   - Expand the chapter by including video tutorials and multimedia content. This can facilitate understanding of preparation techniques and improve the user experience.

5. **Community Engagement:**

   - Create an online forum or social media platform to share experiences, photos, and recipe variations among gelato enthusiasts. This will foster active community engagement.

6. **Adaptation to New Culinary Trends:**

   - Monitor and adapt to new culinary trends, integrating innovative ingredients and creating flavors in line with the expectations of the modern audience.

7. **Exploration of Advanced Production Techniques:**

- Add sections that delve into advanced production techniques, such as using more sophisticated ice cream machines or molecular ice cream techniques, to attract more experienced ice cream enthusiasts.

8. **Promotion of the Unique Experience of Recipes:**

   - Integrate stories and anecdotes related to the recipes, emphasizing the unique experience of each flavor. This can create an emotional connection with customers.

9. **Feedback and Continuous Improvements:**

   - Promote reader participation in providing feedback on the recipes. Use this feedback for continuous improvements and keeping the chapter up-to-date.

10. **Internationalization of Recipes:**

    - Explore international variations of Italian recipes, incorporating culinary influences from other cultures. This can broaden the appeal of the recipes globally.

Projecting the chapter into the future requires a combination of adapting to audience needs, integrating new technologies, and actively engaging the community.

Chapter 15: Collection of Italian Ice Cream Recipes - Events, Courses, and Fairs

Events, Courses, and Fairs:

1. **Thematic Tasting Events:**

   - Organize thematic tasting events at your gelateria. Showcase the recipes from the collection in a welcoming atmosphere, allowing customers to savor the creations and providing detailed information about the recipes.

2. **Participation in Artisanal Ice Cream Fairs:**

   - Participate in artisanal ice cream fairs at regional or national levels. Present the recipes in a dedicated booth, offering free samples and creating networking opportunities with other industry professionals.

3. **Artisanal Ice Cream Course:**

   - Organize artisanal ice cream courses at your gelateria. Use the recipes from the collection as a basis to teach production techniques and present creative variations. Involve enthusiasts and aspiring gelato makers.

4. **Participation in Local Gastronomic Events:**

   - Collaborate with local gastronomic events by offering your creations during themed dinners or food festivals. This can expand the visibility of your gelateria beyond the traditional audience.

5. **Webinars and Online Courses:**

   - Conduct webinars and online courses to reach a wider audience. Use the recipes as a foundation to teach preparation techniques, allowing participants to learn comfortably from home.

6. **Italian Taste Festival:**

   - Participate in or organize an Italian taste festival, showcasing the recipes from the collection alongside other Italian delicacies. This event can attract food enthusiasts and promote Italian gastronomic culture.

7. **Collaborations with Cooking Schools:**

   - Collaborate with local cooking schools to offer gelato courses. Use the recipes as teaching material and involve students in practical preparation.

8. **Gelato Tour in Various Locations:**

   - Organize a gelato tour, bringing your creations to different locations. This can be an opportunity to reach new customers and build connections with diverse communities.

9. **Flavor Creation Contest:**

   - Organize a flavor creation contest, inviting gelato enthusiasts to experiment with the recipes from the collection and submit their variations. Reward winners with incentives like discounts or free products.

10. **Participation in International Ice Cream Events:**

    - Participate in international ice cream events, bringing Italian recipes beyond national borders. This can open up new opportunities and connections in the world of artisanal ice cream.

Integrating events, courses, and fairs into the promotion of the recipes can create an engaging experience for your customers and broaden the visibility of your gelateria

Transforming Your Gelato Shop into a Successful Retail Business

1. **Creation of Packaged Products:**

- *Strategy:* Utilize successful recipes to create packaged products such as ice cream cones, bars, or single-serving jars. Pack your distinctive products carefully, allowing customers to take home the authentic experience of your gelato shop.

2. **Attractive Packaging Design:**

    - *Approach:* Invest in an eye-catching design for the packaging of your packaged products. Attractive packaging can draw buyers' attention and communicate the quality and authenticity of your gelato.

3. **Distribution in Local Grocery Stores:**

    - *Collaboration:* Establish collaborations with local grocery stores to distribute your packaged products. This expands your reach and enables a broader audience to discover the unique flavors of your gelato shop.

4. **Customer Loyalty Program for Retail:**

    - *Incentive:* Implement a customer loyalty program specifically for retail customers. Offer discounts or rewards for frequent buyers, encouraging their loyalty to your brand.

5. **Online Presence and Direct Sales:**

    - *Strategy:* Create a professional website for your gelato shop, offering the option to purchase your products online. This not only increases your visibility but also allows you to reach customers outside your local area.

6. **Participation in Craft Markets:**

    - *Event:* Participate in craft markets or local fairs to sell your packaged products directly. This is an opportunity to interact directly with customers and strengthen the bond with the community.

7. **Exclusivity of Retail Products:**

    - *Strategy:* Introduce occasional exclusive products available only in retail format. This tactic can stimulate demand and create a sense of urgency among customers.

8. **Competitive Pricing Strategy:**

    - *Approach:* Define a competitive pricing strategy for your packaged products. Ensure that the price reflects perceived value and remains accessible to your clientele.

9. **Promotion Through Social Media:**

    - *Channel:* Actively use social media to promote your retail products. Share behind-the-scenes stories, attractive images, and customer testimonials to generate interest and engage your online audience.

10. **Collaborations with Local Influencers:**

- *Collaboration:* Collaborate with local influencers who can promote your packaged products through their platforms. This can expand your online visibility and attract new customers.

Transforming your gelato shop into a successful retail business requires a combination of marketing strategies, smart distribution, and attention to product design and quality.

Glossary of Relevant Terms for Your Gelato Business or Writing Your Books:

1. **Gelateria Artigianale:**

   - A shop or business that produces fresh and high-quality gelato in an artisanal manner, often using natural ingredients.

2. **Edulcorante:**

   - A sweet substance used instead of sugar to impart sweetness to foods and beverages. It can be natural or artificial.

3. **Indice Glicemico:**

   - A scale that measures how a particular food affects blood sugar levels. Foods with a low glycemic index are generally preferred for those with diabetes.

4. **Stevia:**

   - A natural sweetener derived from the leaves of the Stevia plant. It is often used as an alternative to sugar due to its low or zero-calorie content.

5. **Eritritolo:**

- A natural sugar alcohol present in some foods, often used as a low-calorie sweetener.

6. **Vaniglia:**
   - A spice derived from vanilla beans, often used to flavor gelato and other desserts.

7. **Panna Fresca:**
   - Unfermented milk cream with a high fat content, often used in gelato preparation to impart creaminess.

8. **Latte di Mandorle:**
   - Milk obtained from grinding almonds with water, often used as an alternative to cow's milk.

9. **Gelatiera:**
   - An electric appliance used to make gelato. It cools and mixes the gelato base during the freezing process.

10. **Manici Portion Control:**
    - A term that might be relevant in the context of social and volunteer work, referring to practices that allow for fair or controlled distribution of portions.

11. **Marketing del Gusto:**
    - Promotion strategies aimed at highlighting the quality and taste of products, often used to promote gelateries and food products.

Conclusion of "Creating and Managing a Successful Gelateria":

As we reach the end of "Creating and Managing a Successful Gelateria," I hope this manual has not only been an informative guide but also a source of inspiration and passion for the world of gelato. Through these pages, we have explored every aspect, from crafting the perfect base to creating a gelateria that goes beyond a simple dessert.

Your journey into the world of artisanal gelato is a sweet and rewarding one, filled with flavor, creativity, and connection with your community. Whether you are just starting or already established in the industry, I hope the shared knowledge in this manual has equipped you with useful tools to face challenges, discover new horizons, and, above all, delight your customers with extraordinary gelato.

Remember, gelato is more than just a product: it's an experience, a moment of joy and sharing. I hope you carry forward your passion with enthusiasm, continuing to create unique flavors and leaving a positive impact on your community.

Acknowledgments:

In every successful endeavor, there are many people to thank. I would like to express my gratitude to:

- Culinary Inspirations: Those who brought the magic of gelato into our lives, from master gelato makers to producers of high-quality ingredients.

- The Community: Every customer, friend, and community member who supported your gelateria, making it a special place.

- The Team: Passionate individuals working alongside you, contributing with dedication and talent to the creation of extraordinary taste experiences.

- Family and Friends: Those who supported your dream, offering support and encouragement along the way.

- Nature: For the gifts of fresh and delicious ingredients that enrich our gelati.

Finally, a special thank you to you, dear reader, for choosing to explore the world of artisanal gelato through these pages. Whether you are embarking on a new adventure or refining your skills, I wish you all the joy and success that the world of artisanal gelato can offer.

With taste and gratitude, **Nuccio Longardi**

www.ingramcontent.com/pod-product-compliance
Lightning Source LLC
Chambersburg PA
CBHW062347290526
45794CB00005B/2131